AFTER THE HOLOCAUST

by Howard Greenfeld

GREENWILLOW BOOKS
An Imprint of HarperCollinsPublishers

After the Holocaust
Copyright © 2001 by Howard Greenfeld
All rights reserved. No part of this book may be used or reproduced in
any manner whatsoever without written permission except in the case
of brief quotations embodied in critical articles and reviews. Printed in the
United States of America. For information address HarperCollins Children's
Books, a division of HarperCollins Publishers, 1350 Avenue of the
Americas, New York, NY 10019.
www.harperchildrens.com

The photo credits on page 143 are an extension of the copyright page.

The text of this book is set in 11/16 Simoncini Garamond.
Maps by Susan Detrich
Book design by Mina Greenstein

Library of Congress Cataloging-in-Publication Data
Greenfeld, Howard.
After the Holocaust / by Howard Greenfeld.
     p.   cm.
"Greenwillow Books."
Summary: Eight Jewish men and women who survived the Holocaust
as children talk about their experiences immediately following the war.
ISBN 0-688-17752-2 (trade). ISBN 0-06-029420-5 (lib. bdg.)
1. Jewish children in the Holocaust—Biography—Juvenile literature.
2. Holocaust, Jewish (1939–1945)—Juvenile literature.   3. Holocaust
survivors—Biography—Juvenile literature.   4. Refugees, Jewish—
Biography—Juvenile literature.   [1. Holocaust survivors.
2. Holocaust, Jewish (1939–1945)   3. Refugees, Jewish.   4. Jews—
Biography.]   I. Title.
D804.48.G74 2001   940.53'18—dc21   00-052798

1 2 3 4 5 6 7 8 9 10   First Edition

For ANN SHORE,

with gratitude, admiration, and love

Contents

The Children

**CIVIA GELBER
BASCH**

born Oradea Mare,
Romania, 1928

**JUDITH
BIHALY**

born Budapest,
Hungary, 1934

**TONIA ROTKOPF
BLAIR**

born Lodz,
Poland, 1925

**AKIVA
KOHANE**

born Katowice,
Poland, 1929

**LARRY
ROSENBACH**

born Lezajsk,
Poland, 1929

**GEORGE
SCHWAB**

born Liepaja,
Latvia, 1931

**ANN
GOLDMAN
SHORE**

born Zabno,
Poland, 1929

**ALICIA
FAJNSZTEJN
WEINSBERG**

born Warsaw,
Poland, 1929

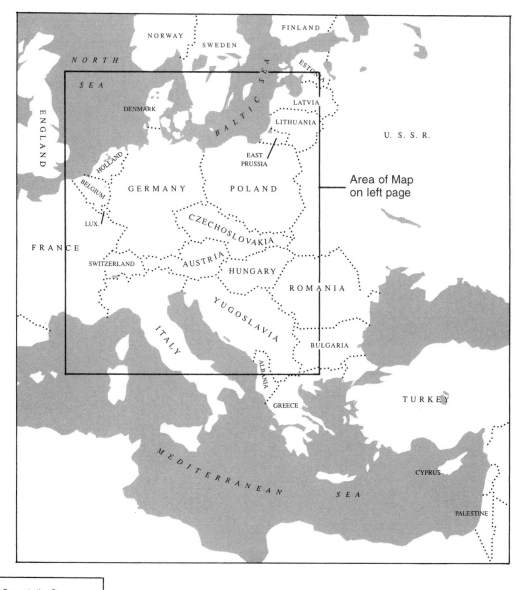

NORWAY
SWEDEN
FINLAND

NORTH
SEA

DENMARK
ESTONIA
LATVIA
LITHUANIA

BALTIC SEA

U. S. S. R.

ENGLAND

HOLLAND
BELGIUM

GERMANY

EAST
PRUSSIA

POLAND

LUX.

CZECHOSLOVAKIA

Area of Map
on left page

FRANCE

SWITZERLAND
AUSTRIA

HUNGARY

ROMANIA

YUGOSLAVIA

ITALY

BULGARIA

ALBANIA

TURKEY

GREECE

MEDITERRANEAN

SEA

CYPRUS

PALESTINE

☐ Concentration Camps
■ Displaced Persons Camps
● Cities
━━ Zone Boundaries
..... Country Boundaries

Europe after World War II

Preface

A few years ago, following the publication of a book I had written about Jewish children who were forced to hide during the Holocaust, I was invited to speak at a number of schools. Most of the students were extraordinarily attentive, and many, in a short time, became emotionally involved in the stories they heard, especially moved by the fact that it was young people, of their own age, who had undergone such suffering. Though some students were either completely ignorant about the Holocaust or, in a few cases, confused and misinformed, a large number knew a great deal about it, and the questions they asked after my talks were, not surprisingly, intelligent and thoughtful.

Curiously, though, no one questioned what had happened to the young survivors of World War II and the Holocaust. They assumed—as most people do, it seems—that the defeat of Hitler and the Nazis somehow, miraculously, brought an end to the suffering of the Jews of Europe.

Unfortunately this was not the case. The years after the Holocaust brought a different kind of suffering to the Jews of Europe. In these pages I will describe, largely through their own words, the period of readjustment and recovery that many thousands of Jews, then teenagers and younger, faced during the years immediately following their liberations and until the time of their departures from Europe, a continent that held too many tragic memories for the majority of them.

The post–World War II experiences of Holocaust survivors have seldom been recorded. Perhaps there is a fear that because the Holocaust was so overwhelmingly and uniquely brutal, they might pale in comparison to the more dramatic experiences that preceded them. This is certainly not so. The post-Holocaust experiences are actually a continuation of the Holocaust itself, not a postscript to it. These survivors suffered not only during the Holocaust but also after it because so many of them were homeless, familyless, adrift, abandoned, and confused. The story of this postwar period must be recorded, since it is an essential chapter in the history of the Holocaust, and must not be forgotten.

A few words of explanation are necessary. Though I interviewed eighteen survivors in order to present a picture of the chaotic years that followed the end of World War II, I have based this book on the testimonies of eight of them. I have done so not because these eight were stronger, more courageous, or more resourceful than the others (or because their stories are more interesting), but because their narratives contain a variety of experiences that, put together, make for a comprehensive picture of this period. (Incidentally, it must be noted that these young people survived not because of strength, courage, or resourcefulness, but only because of luck. They played no significant roles in determining their fates; their persecutors and tormentors did that for them.)

The men and women with whom I spoke currently live in the United States, and I taped my conversations with them over the last two years in or near New York City, in their homes or mine. The eldest was born in 1925, and the youngest in 1934. They all are Jewish. Of course, there were many other victims of the Holocaust: brave non-Jews who joined resistance groups and actively opposed Nazism; at least a quarter of a million Rom, or Gypsies; thousands of homosexuals; men and women who were physically handicapped or, by Hitler's definition, "mentally defective." Their stories must be told, but this book is not about them. This book deals specifically with the experiences of Jewish survivors after the Holocaust.

Those I interviewed spoke to me as adults remembering events and experiences that took place many years ago, under circumstances they would prefer to forget. Their memories are selective. They remember what they want to remember and not what they choose to forget. For example, they all presented an unusually positive picture of life in the displaced persons camps, but it is known that dissatisfied DPs staged many protest demonstrations during their time in the camps.

Memories of details are frequently far from precise or accurate. I have done my best to verify whatever facts I could, but it seems to me relatively unimportant that inconsistencies in dates might remain or that the names of towns and villages and their exact locations may sometimes be mistaken or unknown. What matters is the substance of these moving, unsparingly honest testimonies of their childhoods.

—Howard Greenfeld
New York City, 2001

Liberation

I don't remember any special jumping for joy or things like that. People were in such a situation that they really couldn't care less. . . . We were one-half dead, so the only thing that I was happy about the night that followed was that I didn't have to go back to the barracks, that I could sleep outside.

—Akiva Kohane

We had vodka, and we were drinking and singing, and we were very, very happy. That day my mother said it was actually the first time I was with my parents in the open, because for the last few years we never stayed together outdoors or with other people. My mother, even though I was fourteen years old, she said, "Drink, drink, drink with them."

—Alicia Weinsberg

On May 8, 1945, the Allies—Great Britain, France, the USSR, and the United States—announced the unconditional surrender of Germany. This day, known as V-E Day, marked the formal end of the Second World War in Europe. There would be no more battles, no more bombings, no more useless killings of innocent soldiers or blameless civilians. The defeat of Hitler's army signaled, according to Winston Churchill, the greatest outburst of joy in the history of mankind.

It also marked, informally, the end of the Holocaust. The word *Holocaust* means "destruction by fire" and has come to refer specifically to one of the darkest chapters in history, to when, over a period of more than four years, one nation and its leader, Nazi Germany and Adolf Hitler, tried by all possible means to exterminate the entire Jewish population of Europe—and almost succeeded. The numbers are staggering: There were eight million Jews, and six million of them (approximately the entire population of the state of Massachusetts) were murdered. Among these were one and a half million children who were under the age of sixteen when the war began in 1939.

No exact date can really be assigned to the end of the war or to the end of the Holocaust, for both ended gradually, over a period of several months. During that time, the Allied forces regained the land and power they had been forced to cede to the Germans and their collaborators, and as they did so, the surviving Jews of Europe were liberated.

They were released from the concentration camps in which they had been imprisoned. They were free to leave the mountains and woods where they had risked their lives as partisans, sabotaging the efforts of the enemy forces. Tens of thousands of Jews, many of them youngsters, were finally able to emerge from the hiding places in which they had taken refuge. Some had been hidden in the relative security of convents

Young survivors behind a barbed wire fence in the Buchenwald concentration camp. Buchenwald, Germany. April 11, 1945.

or orphanages or in the homes of courageous non-Jewish families. Others had hidden, often in the most primitive conditions, in forests, haylofts, and basements.

The Jews of Europe had lost the freedom to be educated, to own homes and other possessions, to make livings, to maintain normal social and professional relationships, to have friends . . . and to enjoy themselves. Most of these freedoms might, to some extent and with great difficulty, be slowly recovered. But the young survivors, who had grown to maturity during the years of the Holocaust, had been deprived of one thing that was irretrievably lost: their youth. Moreover, all of them, young and old, having survived an inhuman experience, were to remain scarred for the rest of their lives.

CONCENTRATION CAMPS

The concentration camps, an important feature of the Nazi regime from 1933 to 1945, were used for three major purposes. In the beginning they served as prison camps, where political enemies of the Third Reich were held without any recourse to the judicial process. After a few years, larger camps were set up to serve as prisons for those the Nazis judged to be biologically or racially inferior: the physically or emotionally handicapped, homosexuals, the Rom, or Gypsies, and especially the Jews. In 1939, after the outbreak of the war, the Nazis established hundreds of new camps, in which many of these victims were forced to work on military, industrial, and agricultural projects. As the war effort intensified and the demand for labor increased, the purpose of these camps evolved. Instead of prison camps, a large number of them became forced labor camps and, for those unable to work, killing centers or extermination camps.

More than 3 million people, the majority of them Jews, were murdered in the camps. The largest camp, Auschwitz, was located not far from Kraków, Poland, near the prewar German-Polish border, an area annexed by Germany after its 1939 invasion of Poland. Divided into three parts, Auschwitz functioned as a penal camp (Auschwitz I), an extermination camp (Auschwitz II, or Birkenau), and a forced labor camp (Auschwitz III, or Monowitz). Approximately 1.1 million Jews were killed at Birkenau, which was well known for its four gas chambers into which Jews and other prisoners were crowded and exterminated by the release of the poison gas Zyklon B.

DEATH MARCHES

The death marches were initiated in 1944 and accelerated in the winter of 1945, when the Germans, realizing that they would soon be defeated, tried to erase all trace of their crimes before the approaching Allied forces reached the concentration camps. The Nazis evacuated the camps, getting rid of those prisoners who were able to walk by literally marching them to death. The others were shot before the evacuations began. Long columns of men and women, dressed in striped pajamas and often wearing wooden shoes, were seen lining the highways leading from the camps. A large number of these prisoners were killed by their escorts, while others, allowed no food or water, dropped dead from exhaustion or hunger. Approximately one hundred thousand Jews died while on these marches.

Each of the men and women whose stories are told here experienced liberation in a different place and under different circumstances. They were all innocent victims who had one thing in common: They were young when the Holocaust began.

At the time of their liberation, some were near death in extermination camps or in work camps; it has been reported that of the sixty thousand Jews who walked out of these camps, twenty thousand died within a week. Others were being led from one concentration camp to another on what have become known as death marches. Still others emerged, debilitated and disheartened, from their hiding places.

They responded in different ways upon first learning of their liberation. Some rejoiced—dancing, singing, drinking, kissing, and embracing. Others were too weak or sick to celebrate. They were stunned, too exhausted to comprehend the momentous change that had taken place. None of them was ready to think of or plan for the future. The joys of liberation would, in all cases, be mixed with sadness as the survivors came to realize just how much—families, friends, homes, and communities—they had lost of their past. The joys of liberation would also soon be replaced by the anxieties they would inevitably suffer in the years of decision and readjustment to come.

Ann visiting her grandmother. 1935.

ANN SHORE, born Hania Goldman on April 13, 1929, in Zabno, Poland, was liberated in January 1945, after having spent more than two years hiding with her mother and sister in a tiny lice-infested hayloft not far from her hometown. It was a cramped crawl space without windows or fresh air, and they lived there in constant fear that they would be discovered by the Nazis. This of course would have almost certainly meant death.

Ann was one of the tens of thousands of Jewish children who survived the Holocaust by going into hiding. They became known as "the hidden children." Some of them remained visible. They could be seen on the streets, in town, in the community, but by masking their identities with Christian names and fictitious stories of their past, they managed to hide the fact that they were Jewish. The majority of these hidden children, however, were forced to disappear physically from sight. Many were given refuge in convents or orphanages or were adopted and protected by courageous non-Jewish families. The punishment for hiding Jews was death. Other Jewish children, like Ann, lived for long periods in haylofts, sewers, or airless basements. They all were forced to cope and to mature too quickly, unable to enjoy the pleasures of childhood.

Ann has warm memories of her early years in Zabno:

"It was paradise. The whole town was our playground. During the summer, when the sun was hot, we bathed in the cool river which flowed through our town. We played in the meadows filled with blossoming flowers. And in the winter we skated on the frozen pond and slid down a steep hill. We were always surrounded by laughter and love."

Ann (sitting, left); her sister, Rae (standing, second from right); and friends. The four young people standing were later deported and murdered. Zabno, Poland. 1941.

There was one problem, however: Ann and her family were Jewish, and the non-Jewish residents of the town made no secret of their hatred of the Jewish population. To be Jewish, Ann remembers, was to be less. The Poles felt they had the right to throw stones at them and bombard them with insults. Ann recalls that on one occasion stones were hurled into the front windows of her parents' shoe store. Another time her father was so badly beaten that he came home with blood running down his face.

On September 1, 1939, Hitler's army invaded Poland, signaling the start of the Second World War, and on the seventeenth of that month troops from the Soviet Union, then an ally of Germany, invaded from the east. On the twenty-seventh, Poland surrendered. The Jews of Zabno, and of all Poland, were then officially subject to the Nazis' racial policies and restrictions. Jews were forced to wear armbands with the Jewish Star of David and were not allowed to go more than one and a quarter miles from their towns.

Defiance of these laws was punishable by death. When ten-year-old Ann and her friends went to school wearing their armbands, their classmates made fun of them. At first, they felt degraded, and shortly afterward they were no longer allowed to attend school at all. Ann never forgot one frightening incident. One day, while she was playing out-of-doors, two Nazis on a motorcycle stopped her and demanded to see her armband. Claiming that she was trying to hide it, they beat her brutally. Fortunately, when one asked the other whether he should kill her, he was told that they should let her go. Without looking back, the terrified young girl ran home as fast as she could.

On March 10, 1942, tragedy struck the Jewish population of Zabno. A massacre took place. Thirty Jews were dragged out of their homes, lined up against the wall of a brick factory, and shot. That same night Nazis crashed down the door of the Goldman home, screaming, looking for twelve-year-old Ann's father. They came to the young girl's bed,

Ann's twelfth birthday.
April 13, 1941.

Ann (top left) and a group of children who have just performed a play. All but two were murdered in Belzec. Zabno, Poland. 1941

pressed a gun to her head, and demanded to know where he was. Petrified, she replied that she didn't know. On the way out, they noticed a door to the cellar, where they found him and shot him to death.

"Not long afterwards, in the middle of the night, my mother, my sister, and myself fled from our town, looking for a place to hide. My mother remembered a poor farmer's widow with four children—she used to buy from my parents' shoe store—and we found her farm in the countryside. My mother begged her to give us shelter, and she refused; but, finally, in exchange for money and belongings, she allowed us to hide in a dark hayloft above the house, under a thatched roof.

"After a few months, when we ran out of money and had nothing more to give to the woman, she insisted that we leave. My mother refused, knowing that if we left our hiding place, we would be caught and killed. She let the woman know that she, too, would be killed for giving asylum to a Jewish family. Convinced that she had to save her own skin, she agreed . . . angrily. She became violent, took away the ladder to our hayloft, and broke off all contact with us, except for screaming or cursing at us whenever she caught one of us trying to get down from the hayloft. I was so scared of her that I covered myself with our only tattered goose down cover to drown out her screams."

The only human contact Ann and her family had for more than two years was with three Jewish boys from Zabno, who were also in hiding. They were brave boys, who, though constantly moving from farmer to farmer in search of shelter for themselves, managed to keep in touch with Ann's family. The boys let them know what was happening in the outside world, informing them of the deportations and the mass killings, and sometimes bringing them bread they had obtained from farmers in exchange for eggs Ann had been able to steal. Other than these occasional visits, the family was alone. Ann's only entertainment during these two years was to peer through the slats of the hayloft floor and watch the farm children laugh and play, as she had once done. Everywhere Polish farmers were on the lookout for Jews, hoping to catch them and denounce them to the Germans.

Ann remembers:

"The fear was unbearable at times. When the wind was blowing, we heard sounds from all directions. The rustling of branches and bushes and the barking of dogs always frightened us, and we would stop and listen to hear if someone was coming. We were always on the alert."

Despite the danger of being caught, Ann and her mother—her sister was too sick to help—would climb down from their hayloft in the middle of the night, when the moon had disappeared and the villagers were asleep, to scavenge for food. In time Ann's mother developed a crippling bone disease and could be of little help, so it was the young girl's responsibility to climb trees for fruit, steal vegetables from the fields, steal eggs from the farmers, and gather rotten potatoes from pigsties. It was her job, too, to empty the waste from the bucket they used as a toilet and fill another bucket with water—not clean water from the well, because it had a chain and made noise, but foul-tasting water from a stagnant, algae-covered pond.

In winter life became even more difficult. When the freezing wind penetrated the hayloft, their precious down blanket became covered with a layer of ice. But even then they huddled together under it for warmth. When the pond froze over, and Ann could no longer take water from it, they licked the icicles that hung from the eaves of the roof.

After more than two years from the time they had gone into hiding in the hayloft, the farm woman's brother returned from an army detention camp and helped his sister evict Ann and her family. As miserable as their life had been—they hadn't been out in the daylight, hadn't bathed, and had been afraid to speak above a whisper during that whole period—they had considered themselves lucky to have had a place to hide. Now they were desperate. For several days they roamed the woods until, with the help of the boys who had visited them, they made contact with a sixteen-year-old boy from Zabno who had been hidden by farmers—kindly ones—who had built a shelter for him in their barn. He had lived alone in this straw-covered, rat-infested space for two years. Although there was barely enough room for one person, he let Ann and her family share his hiding place.

Ann continued to go out at night in search of food, but the family's chance of survival seemed slim. Ann's mother was sick and unable to walk. All three of them had bodies swollen from years of malnutrition, and each day their strength diminished. They were sustained only by word that Russian troops were approaching—they themselves heard shelling in the distance—and that the war would soon end. Unfortunately the Russians stopped nearly nineteen miles from their shelter, and they had to spend another six months in hiding.

In January 1945, four months before the war in Europe ended, Ann, her mother, and her sister were finally liberated by the Russians. But there was no joyful celebration—they were too numb and weary for that—or even a feeling of relief, for they were immediately faced with the threat of another tragedy:

"We were warned not to leave our hiding places because the Poles were going to kill the Jews, whoever survived. So we spent another few nights in hiding. The farmer never knew we were there, he didn't know that the three of us were there. We stayed another few nights, and then sometime in January, maybe on the thirteenth, we left the farm in the middle of the night—as many Jews did, so that the nobody in the village would know that a farmer was hiding Jews. This was the greatest disgrace. In many such cases, the farmers were so shamed that they had to leave the villages and move to other places.

"Due to malnutrition, my mother was unable to walk, so the boys who came to help us located a wheelbarrow, put my mother in it, and in the middle of the night we all went back to Zabno. It was the middle of January, the soil was frozen, and we were barely able to push the wheelbarrow. I still remember very vividly how lonely we all looked, my mother curled up so tiny and helpless. If the war had continued another few months, we probably would not have survived. Our bodies were skin and bone, our faces swollen from malnutrition."

ALICIA FAJNSZTEJN WEINSBERG, born in Warsaw on October 2, 1929, had also been in hiding, in the Polish capital, when she was liberated in September 1944.

Her childhood was, in her own words, "absolutely perfect." The

Alicia and her cousin at their summer house outside Warsaw, Poland. 1938(?).

immediate family, which consisted of Alicia, her parents, and her younger sister, Sophie, was very close, and they especially enjoyed summers in a country house outside Warsaw, where they were joined by members of their large extended family.

As Jews they were separated from the rest of the Polish population, but they were accustomed to this form of anti-Semitism and had looked upon it as normal. During the summer of 1939, however, there were indications that, with the passage of harsh anti-Semitic laws in Poland, it would be best for the Jews of Poland to leave their country. Alicia's family considered making a move, but her strong-willed grandfather vigorously opposed the idea.

By September 1, 1939, when German forces invaded Poland, it was too late. Toward the end of the month, after a number of heavy air attacks and artillery bombardments, Warsaw surrendered, and the following day Germany and the Soviet Union formally divided the country, with the Germans occupying the west and the Soviet Union the eastern part. (Less than two years later, on June 22, 1941, Germany invaded the Soviet Union, breaking their alliance, and annexed eastern Poland.)

Alicia's false papers. 1944.

The word *ghetto* comes from the Italian; it described the area of Venice in which Jews were required to live during the sixteenth century.

Between 1939 and 1942 the Nazis established numerous ghettos, most of them in Eastern Europe. Shortly after they occupied Poland, the Nazis formed several of these enclosed quarters within a number of Polish cities. The two largest were in Warsaw and Lodz. The purpose of the ghettos was to segregate and isolate the Jews from the population at large, so that they might be more easily controlled and eventually deported to death camps or labor camps. The Jews of the Warsaw ghetto lived under the most miserable conditions, characterized by overcrowding (30 percent of the city's population was contained within 2.4 percent of its land), disease, a serious shortage of sanitary facilities, and, frequently, starvation. While some of the ghettos were enclosed by wooden fences

Life would never again be the same for any of Warsaw's 375,000 Jews. Alicia and her family were moved by the authorities from apartment to apartment until October 1940, when the Germans announced the establishment of the Warsaw ghetto.

Alicia remembers the family's first month in the ghetto as "not very, very bad." They were relatively lucky. Although they had a limited supply of food, they were not starving, and although they had no bathroom, they did have a portable toilet. Furthermore, in spite of a curfew, it was even possible for Alicia to leave the ghetto from time to time, though to do so, she had to walk through piles of corpses, victims of disease or starvation. Most important, and what made life bearable for Alicia, was the fact that the entire family could be together.

All this changed on November 16, 1940, when the ghetto was officially sealed, and the eleven-year-old girl was no longer able to move about freely. Nonetheless, her family remained among the very few fortunate ones. Food was available for money, and the family had money as well as a vegetable garden. They were able to observe the Jewish holidays, and Alicia could attend a decent school within the ghetto walls. Incredibly, they even had a Jewish girl who served as a maid and did the cooking and cleaning while Alicia and her parents were at work (Alicia found a job in a factory where uniforms were made for German soldiers). But Alicia's family was the exception. In 1941, one out of every ten residents of the Warsaw ghetto died from disease, malnutrition, or exposure to the cold.

During the summer of the following year, 1942, the Germans began to empty the ghetto, gradually rounding up more than 300,000 Jews and moving them to the Umschlagplatz, the deportation point. Though some of the Jews believed they were being sent from there to work camps, it was soon clear that they were to be transported in cattle cars from the Umschlagplatz to Treblinka, an extermination camp sixty miles from Warsaw. In a short time only fifty-five thousand Jews, including

or barbed wire, the one in Warsaw, the largest of all, was surrounded by eleven miles of nine-foot-high walls.

Approximately 80,000 out of 445,000 Jews died in the Warsaw ghetto, while 45,000 out of 200,000 Jews died in Lodz.

When these ghettos were dissolved, the surviving Jews were rounded up and sent to concentration camps, where the majority of them lost their lives.

Alicia and her family, who miraculously avoided being chosen for deportation, remained in the ghetto. The family realized, though, that their luck could not last and that they would have to leave the ghetto on their own to avoid being taken to the deportation point.

On January 19, 1943, they decided to make their move. Having learned that another large roundup of Jews was imminent, they escaped by simply walking through one of the gates before nine o'clock, when the gates were locked. Alicia's father, she believes, must have bribed one of the guards.

Finding a way to leave the ghetto was not impossible, but deciding what to do next posed another, and perhaps greater, problem. For Alicia and her family, the deprivations, fears, and horrors of life in the ghetto were replaced by the anxieties, uncertainties, and dangers of life outside it, in a city inhabited by hostile Poles and Germans.

Life outside the ghetto proved to be even more harrowing for the thirteen-year-old girl than life inside it had been. She obtained false papers with the help of Joseph Biczyk, the superintendent of the apartment house in which the family had formerly lived, who was willing to risk his own life to save that of the young girl. These documents identified her as a non-Jew, enabling her to live in the open as a Christian relative of the Biczyk family.

This period of unexpected freedom, however, soon came to an end. Because of fears that she might be discovered, Alicia was forced to leave.

Alicia (top) and her sister with Helene and Joseph Biczyk. Warsaw, Poland. 1943.

It was a difficult time, as she moved frequently, hiding in building after building, sometimes with one or both of her parents and sometimes alone, wondering where her parents were and if she would ever see them again. For several months she lived in the country, acting as companion to an old woman who gave her so little to eat that the frightened girl had to steal vegetables from the woman's garden. When she returned to Warsaw, she was again helped by Joseph Biczyk and his family, who had already taken in Alicia's younger sister and treated her as they would have their own child.

These were chaotic times in Warsaw. In August 1944 members of the Polish underground rose up against the German occupation forces. Tens of thousands of Poles were killed. Meanwhile the Soviet Army waited on the outskirts of the city, militarily able to enter the capital but unwilling to do so since such a move would have aided the Polish rebels, whom they hated more than they hated the Germans.

Alicia remembers her liberation on September 4 and the days preceding it:

"We—by that I mean my sister, myself, and the people that were hiding us, and at that time I was with my parents and my aunt—we had to leave the house where we were hiding and living because it was very close to the front. We were expecting them to blow up the whole building, so we had to move out and find a place to spend the last days or weeks; we didn't know how long it would take before the Russian Army would come, but they were very close. They were thirty or forty kilometers [more than twenty miles] from where we were. But you never knew how long it would take. So we ventured out and the first two nights we had no place to be, and so we spent the nights at a Catholic cemetery. It turned out to be one of the biggest cemeteries in Europe—I didn't know it at the time—but we spent two nights there hiding. And it was terrible because there were so many bugs—we were bitten by mosquitoes—and we were afraid they would find us because they were putting these big lights over the cemetery. Anyway, a place was found for my mother and another place was found for my father, and we stayed in this Polish family's relatives' house. And as the front was coming they were bombing around and they burned that house also. So we jumped out of the windows and threw out everything we could save for those people, and we were actually on the street—in the field, because it was outside, on the outskirts of Warsaw. And we moved to another house which was a small apartment building, and the bombardment was terrible, but I refused to go to the basement, and I said, 'I am sleeping in my bed or not sleeping, but I refuse to hide anymore, I can't stand it.'

"These were the last few days, and a day or two before, Germans got hold of me. They, of course, didn't know I was Jewish, but they were looking for young girls, women, and they brought us to a building where they gave us things to wash and darn and clean, and I think they had something else in mind also. . . . But before anything happened, the bombardment started and they jumped in their cars—they found their cars in a rush—this was like a day or two before liberation. And then we just were sitting in the field because we could hear the armament and bombs being—the explosions, very, very nearby. And, I think, the day after, the tanks started coming. And we were between the villages—so it was mostly fields—and everybody was watching the narrow road when the tanks started pouring in—the Russian tanks. And we were greeting them with flowers. It was September, so we still had field flowers, and we were crying, and they were terribly happy to meet us. They were sitting on the tanks and moving, and the next day, of course, that whole part of Warsaw, Praga, was liberated.

"And we could pick up our parents. First, my father, who hadn't been on the street for a long time, and my mother and my aunt. And we went back to the building where we were hiding—by that time, a day later, it was full of Russians. The building had been empty because the Germans left it like a ruin—they already had a chance to plunder everything. In the basement where we hid our clothing, everything was scattered all over staircases in the building. I don't know how they found it. It was hidden under piles of wood and bricks. The Russians came to the kitchen, and we had vodka and we were drinking and singing, and we were very, very happy. That day my mother said it was actually the first time I was with my parents in the open, because for the last few years we never stayed together outdoors or with other people. But my mother, even though I was fourteen years old, she said, 'Drink, drink, drink with them.' Oh, I knew how to drink. I knew how to drink at that time, it was unbelievable how much I was used to drinking vodka. I had learned, being of good Polish people, to drink enormous amounts of alcohol. Actually, it was a home brew of vodka, and sometimes it was very bad, but we were drinking. . . ."

JUDITH BIHALY was liberated while staying at a large villa in or near Budapest, Hungary—she is not sure of the exact location—in late December 1944. She had been hidden not only during the war, but even before it. Though she had remained physically visible, and had not been among the many Jewish children who had been forced to disappear from sight, her identity had been masked and her Jewishness hidden for much of her life.

Judith and her twin brother, Andrew, at the wedding of their cousin Magda to Imre. Both the bride and groom perished. Hungary. 1939.

She was born in Hungary on December 16, 1934. Her family, completely assimilated, was part of the Christian community. (This would have been impossible or, at best, extremely difficult in Poland.) Her parents were too busy to pay much attention to Judith and her twin brother, Andrew, and after the age of two, the children were sent to day care and nursery schools and then later to the countryside or to the suburbs, where they lived with relatives or, at times, with strangers.

At the age of six the children were baptized; this amounted to a conversion, though Judith never imagined that there was a time when she wasn't Catholic.

When they were nine years old, Judith and her brother returned to their parents' home in Budapest. It was not a happy family. Her father, a dentist, and her mother, a dressmaker, were estranged. Judith and her brother were not close, and the young girl found consolation and peace only in the Catholic Church—in the beauty of the mass, the music, and the rituals, which were such a familiar part of her life. Until March 1944 she never questioned her identity as a Catholic.

The successes of the Nazis between 1938 and 1941 had convinced the Hungarian government to join the Nazi cause, and it entered the war against the Soviet Union in June 1941. While Jews in the rest of Nazi-dominated Europe were being systematically destroyed as part of Hitler's Final Solution, the situation in Hungary was unique. Though deprived of basic civil and economic rights and separated socially from the rest of the population, the 825,000 Hungarian Jews continued to enjoy a relatively tranquil life.

All this changed abruptly in early 1944, when the Germans, having learned that the Hungarians were holding secret negotiations to join the Allied cause, invaded Hungary. Judith remembers the day the Germans marched into Budapest. It was March 19, 1944, and she mistakenly believed she was witnessing a momentous victory for her people.

"I was on the boulevard. I remember the tanks and the infantry and the cavalry and the trucks going up and marching up the boulevard. I remember this humongous throng of people. The strange thing is I don't remember specifically what these people did, except that I remember walking up to my apartment and feeling completely elated. So energized! I imagine what must have happened on the street may have been people throwing flowers and singing and such. I don't remember the specifics, but I remember the feeling of elation. I walked to our apartment, and I remember my mother was at the window looking out towards this railroad station where the marching had taken place. She was holding this curtain with her finger like this, as if she wanted to peer out. She didn't want to expose herself. I was full of energy, and I remember saying to her so enthusiastically, 'Isn't this a wonderful day? What a glorious day! Now we can start killing all the Jews.' My mother turned around and I could see that her face was totally white. There was no blood in her face at all. I knew I said something wrong. I asked, 'What did I say?' It took my mother a long time to answer. Then she said, 'Your grandmother was born Jewish. You are never to say anything about that.' My grandmother was born Jewish. I was never to say anything about that. . . . That was the first time I heard my mother say the word *Jew*."

From that day Judith gradually, but with great difficulty, attempted to shed her identity as a Catholic. She failed to understand why her world and her place in it were changing so radically, but not yet ten years old, she asked no questions. Although she was disturbed and puzzled, she was reluctantly forced to accept the fact that because her grandmother was Jewish, she was no longer considered a Catholic and that, on the few occasions she left her home, she had to wear the yellow star that marked her as a Jew.

The world around her was changing as well. In Budapest thousands of apartments occupied by Jews were confiscated, and their inhabitants were rounded up and interned in camps around the capital. Throughout the rest of the country Jews were forced to leave their property behind and live in crowded ghettos. Sensing that Germany would soon lose the war, the Nazis hurried to complete their task—to annihilate what was left of the Jewish population in Hungary—before it was too late. They were remarkably efficient. On May 15, 1944, massive deportations began, and by July 8 almost 440,000 Jews had been deported to the concentration camp at Auschwitz. With the exception of the Jews of Budapest, who were temporarily spared this fate when the deportations were suspended in July, Hungary was by then free of Jews. What it had taken the Germans and the Poles years to accomplish, the Nazis and their Hungarian collaborators were able to do in a mere fifty-four days.

Not long after the start of the German occupation, Judith's mother, in an attempt to make the authorities believe her daughter was not Jewish, sent her to a Catholic residential school. There she and the other girls, most of them older, learned household skills—cooking, sewing, gardening, and caring for animals—and there, as her mother had wished, her identification with Catholicism was renewed and intensified. Judith believes today that she never lost or changed her identity because she had never really had one.

Judith remembers that there were frightening air raids; the Soviets were pounding Budapest with bombs during the spring of 1944. She remembers the horror and the fact that she never questioned the reasons for the destruction. Along with other children, she was moved from place to place, never knowing why and never participating in any decision. She merely did what she was told to do. She felt that she was escaping, but why . . . and from what? Finally, she was in a villa, several stories high, on a large property with a number of children. Her memories of her stay there are vague. She shared a bunk bed with another girl in a very crowded room, and she recalls that the young people there spoke of nothing but food. This was a joyous topic, and they recalled past meals with pleasure. But Judith found the food offered to her at the villa unappetizing and barely edible. Conditions there were for the most part terrible. The septic system didn't work, so the toilet couldn't be used, which meant long walks in the snow to an outhouse, a painful experience since the soles of Judith's shoes were worn out.

Though Judith was of course unaware of this at the time, the Jews of Budapest were during this period bearing the brunt of the Nazi wrath. In October 1944, with the Soviet Army only 120 miles from the capital and capable of surrounding it at any time, the Germans installed a viciously anti-Semitic Hungarian government that, intent on exterminating the last Jews before the war came to an end, instituted a reign of terror in Budapest. Thousands of Jews were taken to the banks of the Danube, where they were shot and thrown into the river. Deportations resumed, and Jews were sent to concentration camps in Austria and Germany; many thousands were shot along the way, and thousands more died from starvation or from the freezing cold.

In November the remaining Jews of Budapest were removed from their homes and sent to a ghetto. Crammed into small spaces, thirteen or fourteen to a room, many died. Finally, by late December, Soviet troops had completed a blockade of the city. Judith remembers her liberation:

"One day, I heard someone remark that it was Christmas morning. As we were talking, an adult hushed us because she thought she heard someone speak Russian. All of us fell silent. There were no sounds of bombs or shooting. After a while, the Russian soldiers came into the building. We must have been a terrible sight, with runny noses, heads full of lice, starved, and wearing filthy, smelly clothes, but when they saw us, they picked us up, hugged us, and held us. That's why I've never been able to hate the Russian occupiers the way most Hungarians did. They brought us big piles of apples to eat. Someone said that the Russians found a bunker full of pro-German Hungarian soldiers on the grounds outside our building and used flamethrowers to kill them all. That's where they found the store of apples.

"The Russians used our grounds to execute German prisoners who had tried to escape. The prisoners were being marched up this big boulevard on the property where we were, and anytime any of them tried to run away, the Russians would bring them to our property to shoot them to death. I wouldn't look out the window, because I remembered my mother saying that children should never be allowed to see a dead body. So I wouldn't look, but other kids were looking out the window and giving play-by-play reports."

Though she was unable to comprehend exactly what had happened, Judith realized—largely because of the presence of the Russians—that for her the war had ended:

"I remember once smelling this wonderful smell of corn roasting in the fire, and I wanted to know where the corn came from. It was still on the cob, and it was one of these dry corns, the kind you feed to livestock. One of the kids said that there was a whole pile outside where the Russians were feeding their horses with it. I remember going out to see where this was, because all these kids were helping themselves to it. When I was about to take a cob, my feeling was a mixture of guilt and fear. I remember a horse looking at me with big, sad eyes—

because the corn was his—and feeling guilty and not being able to steal, because it meant stealing corn from the horse. I smelled it, and it smelled delicious. . . .

"Anyway, one day I remember hearing that everything was over. The Pest side of Budapest was free. I'm not sure how much later, but they loaded us into wagons, horse-drawn wagons. We were riding down the hill, approaching the Danube, and there were pontoon bridges because all the bridges had been bombed out. This man was driving the horses with us in the wagon, and as we reached the Danube, I remember the man saying, pointing to the shore, 'This is where they used to take you kids to be shot into the Danube.' All the kids in the wagon let off a big gasp, because we remembered how people— we didn't know who they were—used to come from time to time and say to us, 'We found new homes for ten of you.' I think we were all under the impression that we were kept there while people were trying to find homes for us. I remember how all of us kids were jumping and saying, 'Take me, take me.' Now we realized that the kids chosen were taken to the side of the Danube to be shot into it. . . ."

GEORGE SCHWAB was born in November 1931 in Liepaja, a city of some hundred thousand people in southwestern Latvia. He was liberated in May 1945, while on a journey to a German death camp.

Latvia, once an independent state, had been annexed by the Soviet Union in 1940. The following year, after the German invasion of the Soviet Union, the Nazis occupied the country. Anti-Semitism was rampant. That was nothing new. The Latvians had long hated the ninety-five thousand Jews who lived in their country—but now that anti-Semitism intensified. Jews were robbed and beaten by both Germans and Lat-

Saying good-bye to a cousin who is leaving for America. George is the little boy in the middle. Liepaja, Latvia. 1936.

vians, and their apartments were searched for family treasures as part of a state policy of plundering Jewish property for the Nazis. The Schwab apartment was one of those plundered, and in the summer of 1941 George's father, a prominent gastroenterologist, was arrested and hauled off to prison, where he was tortured and murdered. Months later, in December 1941, the Jewish population was divided into two groups: those who were assigned to forced labor camps and those who were to be taken and killed. Most were killed. Because she had obtained a safety pass, George's mother managed to save herself, George, and George's older brother.

In the summer of 1942 the Schwabs and other Jewish residents of the larger cities were moved to ghettos, where they were fenced off by barbed wire and patrolled by black-uniformed Latvian guards. By the beginning of 1943 only five thousand Jews remained in Latvia.

In October 1943 the Liepaja ghetto was dissolved, and the Schwabs were among those packed into cattle cars and shipped to the capital city of Riga. They were then taken to the nearby Kaiserwald labor camp.

At first George worked, in the bitter cold, at an oil storage depot. He then bribed his way to a railroad camp, where his brother worked under improved conditions: It was warmer, sanitary facilities were better, and there were fewer beatings. When word spread that Germany was losing the war, morale improved, but only until July 1944, when there was another "selection." Eight hundred inmates were ordered to undress and pass before three German officers, who sent some of them to the left and others to the right. George was chased back to camp, while his brother was sent in the opposite direction to his death.

It was about a week later that George, together with Jewish and non-Jewish prisoners from all over Europe, was placed on a cargo ship at Riga, headed for concentration camps throughout Germany. By coincidence, he was on the same ship as his mother; but when they reached the port of Danzig, in Poland, they were separated and sent to different camps. This was in August 1944: George, only twelve years old, was alone.

His final destination was the concentration camp at Stutthof, twenty-two miles east of Danzig. Stutthof had once been a civilian internment camp. It then became a special SS camp, and in January 1942 it became a concentration camp. Surrounded by electrified barbed wire fences, it was staffed by SS men and Ukrainian auxiliaries; most of the guards, many of them former criminals, were Germans.

Conditions at the camp were brutal. A number of prisoners were beaten to death by the guards, while others were worked to death. Still others, victims of primitive sanitary conditions, succumbed to dysentery or typhoid. The food was inadequate and barely edible. George recalls:

"During the day, we had two cups of coffee. One in the morning. It was very watery. No milk or—sometimes a little sugar, but it was a brown sugar, not white sugar. In the morning we also received a moldy piece of bread. The combination of a moldy piece of bread, sugar, and coffee, we always had the runs. There were hardly any toilet facilities. Lunchtime we had a kind of soup, if you could call it that, and the lineup was very important. It came in large canisters, the soup.

On top the soup was watery. If you could line up a little bit near the end, you would get what was at the bottom of the soup. Some potatoes, maybe a piece of horsemeat or other kind of meat. Maybe some rice at the bottom. Of course, it was just very little, but we ate it as if it was the greatest delicacy."

In late April 1945, as the Soviet Army advanced and Stutthof was about to be encircled, George and some forty-five hundred other prisoners were removed from the camp and shipped by barges to the German port of Hamburg. Each prisoner was given just one piece of bread, and there was nothing to drink but seawater—for a journey that lasted seven days. Many died under these circumstances, and approximately two thousand more either drowned or were shot by the Nazis while at sea.

But the surviving prisoners never disembarked at Hamburg. Upon learning that the British Army had already arrived there, the guards towed the barges to a mined area in the Baltic Sea, three miles from the coastal town of Neustadt in Holstein, and abandoned their prisoners on the high seas while they themselves fled during the night. The following morning, May 3, with sails made from blankets by resourceful Scandinavian prisoners of war, the weary, debilitated men managed to sail the barges through the minefields to the coast.

"We had to wade to shore, and I was—after seven days of having nothing but seawater, saltwater—I was swollen because of hunger. I wanted to be left alone, but a friend of the family was there, a good family friend, and he said no. 'As long as I'm going to be alive, you're going to be alive.' He dragged me through the water early in the morning. There were no guards, nothing at all. Suddenly, when we were already ashore, though

The wreck of the Cap Arcona. The Cap Arcona was attacked and destroyed by four squadrons of British Typhoon fighters on May 3, 1945. Neustadt in Holstein, Germany.

a good number of people were still coming ashore, suddenly German naval personnel, sailors, arrived on the scene. They started shooting indiscriminately; well, I won't say indiscriminately. First of all, at people who were still wading from the barges to the shore and those who were too weak to walk. They were just shooting. The rest of us who could still walk did, although I begged this family friend to leave me alone. I had absolutely no strength left, and he had swollen legs because he had been bitten by dogs—by police dogs—in Stutthof. He just sort of took me by the collar and pretty much dragged me, though he himself had no strength left."

Once on land, George and the others were led by German sailors on a two-mile march to a large naval base, formerly a U-boat school, in Neustadt. There two ships, the *Cap Arcona* and the *Thielbek*, were embarking thousands of prisoners, moving them to other locations just ahead of the Allied advance. Among these were hundreds of Jews who had been evacuated from Stutthof and were being taken out in small boats to be put on the ships. George was one of those who was to be put aboard the *Cap Arcona*, but by the time he arrived at the ship, the captain was refusing to take any more passengers—there were already seventy-five hundred Jews on board—and the small boats were ordered back to shore without unloading their passengers. The boy's life had been miraculously saved: British planes, whose pilots were unaware that the *Cap Arcona* was carrying concentration camp prisoners, attacked and sank the ship in Lübeck Bay—and only a few hours later the fortunate prisoners who had been unable to board it were freed, at the naval base, by British soldiers.

George Schwab remembers how he learned of his liberation:

"I was utterly starved. I was looking around in garbage pails, looking around, and suddenly I saw a German soldier standing there and I didn't even realize that he didn't have a rifle, and there was a lot of stuff. I walked over, and I picked up a piece of soap, thinking it was bread. I started to bite but I couldn't bite because it was soap. I guess I hallucinated. Then I walked over to him and asked him in German if I could have a slice of bread. He said, 'Why don't you walk over there to the tank? These are Americans.' (They were actually British. He didn't know that.) 'These are Americans, and he will give you some bread.'

"I looked at him, and there were rifles, there were pistols. I picked up a pistol; I thought maybe I should shoot him. I picked it up. I didn't know how to handle it. But then there was something that made me put it down, that I couldn't even, if I had known how to shoot, I don't think I would have had the nerve to shoot a human being. I stumbled over to the tank which was forty or fifty yards away, and I was fortunate. I had had a British tutoress as a child, so English was not really an alien language to me. I asked him, 'May I please have a slice of bread? I'm very hungry.' He gave me tea cookies. The soldier in the tank had these little cans . . . gave me a few cookies. That was how I knew I was liberated."

LARRY ROSENBACH was liberated on April 23, 1945, while on a death march from Flossenburg to Dachau.

Born on April 2, 1929 (though he believes that the real date of his birth was that of his liberation), in the small town of Lezajsk, Poland, Larry had had a happy childhood. His father, an honorable and generous man, who had a good job in a lumberyard, was a loving father, and his mother was devoted to and protective of both Larry and his older brother, Arthur. The family was not religious and rarely attended synagogue services, but they were Zionists, who enthusiastically endorsed and often spoke of the establishment of a Jewish state in Palestine. Although they had no social dealings with non-Jewish Poles, Larry's father worked with and maintained professional relationships with them. On the whole, they were aware of anti-Semitism, but they did not feel oppressed by it.

Among the onerous restrictions imposed upon the Jews following the Nazi occupation in September 1939 was one that particularly upset Larry: Jews would no longer be allowed to attend school. This meant the end of the ten-year-old boy's education. Worst of all, the Germans began massive deportations of Jews, Larry's father among them.

At the end of 1942 Larry himself was taken from his home in Poland and sent to a number of relatively small work camps, including the notoriously harsh facility at Budzyn. He survived only by convincing himself that he was living through a nightmare from which he would soon awaken, just as his mother had promised him that the frightening *Grimm's Fairy Tales* she had given him to read would end and all would be well.

In the fall of 1944 the Germans began to liquidate these small camps and send the prisoners to larger camps throughout Poland and Germany. In early 1945 sixteen-year-old Larry was sent to such a camp, at Flossenburg, in southern Germany, only a few miles from the Czech border. It was there, sometime in March, that his death march began: Some

Top: Larry's grandfather. Undated.

Bottom: Larry's grandmother. 1889.

Larry at Hebrew School. Undated.

twenty thousand prisoners, about 10 percent of them Jewish, were awakened in the middle of the night and hurriedly taken to the local railroad station, where they were loaded onto trains for a journey to another large camp at Dachau, some two hundred miles to the south. In the midst of the trip, the cars that carried the prisoners were attacked by British fighter planes. The pilots believed the train was transporting German soldiers.

Larry remembers:

"They started shooting at us, and thirty-five of us got wounded. We started to jump from the trains and hide, run. And the SS were hiding among us because we had striped uniforms— they thought maybe it was safe to hide among us. And some guys took advantage of this, and they went up to get the SS supplies, their food, bread. And they robbed whatever food they could, and they ate it up. I remember one guy. He ripped a piece

Left: Larry (center), his brother, and his mother on vacation in Rabka, Poland. 1937.

Below, from left to right: Larry's uncle, brother, mother, Larry, and Larry's father on vacation. Zaklikow, Poland. 1938.

of bread, and he was starting to eat it, and another guy came and went to grab a piece from him, and the one who wanted to grab the piece got a bullet just when they were fighting over the bread, got a bullet in his throat. Blood splashed on the bread, and the other guy ate it up with the blood, and this guy fell. The one that fell was my friend, and he didn't die; he was wounded. In all, thirty-five of us were wounded."

The wounded were placed on the train, and both the journey and the intermittent attacks by the British aircraft resumed. By the time the train reached the nearby town of Schwarzenfeld, its engine had been disabled, and it was clear that the rest of the journey had to be taken on foot. The SS men removed the wounded from the train, piled them up, sprayed gasoline over them, and burned them. Other prisoners who were unable to walk were also murdered.

The surviving prisoners walked during the daytime and rested in the forest at night. Those who dropped out of the formation were shot and thrown into ditches. Except for a half loaf of bread, thrown at the prisoners by a woman who watched them pass by, and some raw potatoes found along the way, there was no food.

"The last few days it was pouring all the time at night, and it was cold rain, almost like snow. We were all cold and wet and soaked. The guards were also wet, so they chased us into a yard and closed us in this yard, while they went to change clothes and to warm up and to take a shower, I guess, inside the farmhouse. And they left us in the yard. So I looked around and saw that there was a pigsty, so I sneaked in over there, and I saw a pig standing over a trough eating his food. I joined him and I started to take food with my hands from the trough and eat. After a while, somebody else noticed, and they started to come in. They stood in front of the trough and everybody was helping himself. After a few minutes, the trough was empty—licked out. I wasn't hungry because I had filled up. . . . So I looked around; I happened to look at the pig. He was staring because he remained with no food and couldn't understand what was going on. So he was staring, and it made me laugh.

"We proceeded further till early in the morning when we reached a small village. We were all soaked and wet, and I had a headache. They chased us into a barn where there was straw; the whole floor was covered with three feet deep of straw. And one group of people came in, they lay down, and they were cold so they covered themselves with a layer of straw. Another group came in, and they lay down on top of them. So there were two layers of people, because everybody was so exhausted they didn't even have the time to prepare a good place, they just dropped in the straw. And my brother, who had been with me, and I and a few others saw an alcove in this barn, and I figured I wouldn't lie down here on the bottom—there was hay in the alcove, not straw. So we climbed up there, and we lay down in the hay and we had private quarters there, just the six of us. We were contemplating—because we were hidden—staying there. We figured we'd hide there and remain. But we didn't know the situation, where is the front, where are the Americans, where are the Germans? We didn't know how far we were.

"But anyway, in the morning as we were hiding in this alcove, the Germans came into the barn and yelled, 'Everybody out, out, out.' And they were really in a hurry and rushing and a lot of people got up and they formed in front of the barn, and we were still in the alcove—we didn't move. But after a few

Larry after liberation. 1945.

minutes a German came in with a rifle and a bayonet and was standing like this, and he was poking the straw, and we heard some screams, they got some people with the bayonet. And some people were packing up, and the ones that didn't try to hide there—or maybe they were sleeping—were packing up and running out. So we changed our minds. We decided to jump down and also go out because we were afraid they would catch us there and shoot us.

"We made a formation and went into the forest, and we were walking on this road in the forest, and everybody was at the end—we got so wet and cold and lay down. I had a headache, I couldn't see out of my eyes. My head was bursting. If we would have to go another mile, I wouldn't make it anymore. And really in this mile that we walked in the forest, maybe a third of us dropped. They were all so exhausted. Many of my friends dropped out then. And after we walked like this for maybe half an hour or an hour in the forest, all of a sudden the people in front of me stopped, just like sheep, one after another, we didn't care where we were going, what we were doing, you know, just put the head down and we were just walking. So while the formation came to a stop and we were standing like this for ten minutes, fifteen minutes, half an hour, and nothing was happening so we were all thinking the same thing, that they probably had surrounded us, they were making preparations, they would kill us all now.

"I took five guys from my group, we were all young boys, and I became the leader and organized them. I said, 'Listen, let's leave the formation and work our way as far away as we can away from the formation. And they will be shooting, so we will go lie down over there and maybe they won't miss us.' They listened and we went away maybe fifty yards from the formation, and we lay down and it was raining, it was wet, we had blankets which were also soaking wet. We were lying there maybe for a few hours, resting, sleeping, I don't know. And nothing was happening. So I said, 'Listen, let's start walking.' But the decision that they made was to walk in the direction from which they came, because we didn't know what direction to go. We can wind up with the German Army. We started to walk towards the village, where the barn was which we were sleeping in during the night.

"We came out of the forest to a clearing, there was a plane circling us. I think it was an American plane. And we were scared to go through the clearing so they shouldn't see us. Because we didn't know if it was German or American. But we made it through the clearing and then through another piece of forest. So we made it out of the forest maybe a few hundred feet from the first houses in the village and we were walking, and we see one of our guards running towards us. So we thought, that's it, now they got us and we will be killed. And we couldn't run because we were hardly able to walk. He came closer and closer to us, and we were counting the minutes that we were going to be killed. He came to us, and he says, in German, he says, 'Did you eat already something?' We looked at him and said no, no. He says, 'Go into the school—there is a school in the village, and you will get something to eat over there.' He talked so nice to us that we couldn't believe our ears. He was by himself, there were five of us, he was probably scared that we might do something to him. From the back he will kill us. That was my thought. So when he passed us by I looked around and I figured now I have to die, because bullets were flying. But no, he ran further. I just looked around, and he was running further. I couldn't understand what was going on.

"We proceeded but we didn't know whether to go to this school where he told us, because we thought again maybe they would gather us and do something. But we went to the first house on the edge of the village, and a woman gave us each one a boiled potato and a piece of bread. I took it in my mouth, I figured I would eat up, devour it, but I couldn't swallow it. I put in the bread but I couldn't swallow it. Everything was dried out inside me. But I wouldn't refuse the bread and the potato. . . . I had a rope around my waist, and I put it like above the rope. And we go further, and another woman from a different house again, she gives us bread and potatoes. I gathered the two pieces of bread and the potatoes, and I put it all there. And we were walking like this behind the barns because we were afraid to go on the road. Behind the barns there were fields and we were walking in the fields. And we didn't know what direction to go, where to go; we were just walking. Then it came to my mind that I had to look for someone to ask where are the Americans, where is the front, maybe we are. . . . This was in the evening. When it will get dark we will know where to proceed and how to get closer to them and not to go in the wrong direction. But I was afraid to ask this woman because they might accuse me of—that I am a traitor or a spy or something else, and they might beat me up and then shoot me. So I was waiting for a chance to ask somebody and all of a sudden from a distance I saw an old German guy who was all bent and he was gray with a long beard, coming out of the barn, into the fields, walking slowly. So I told the guys to lie down there in the fields—I think there were beets growing, but there was a place to hide. And I went over to him—it was maybe one hundred yards—and I said, 'Tell me something'—I was afraid even of him, but I figured I would stand a distance from him so if he went to catch me I would run away from him because he was walking very slowly. I said, 'Where are the Americans, where is the front, which direction?' I pointed. 'Where are the Americans?' He said, 'There's no more German Army over here. The Americans passed by here this morning.' I was so excited I almost jumped at him and kissed him and hugged him. I was so happy with this, what he told me. And I ran over to the guys and said, 'Guys, we are liberated. The Americans are here already.' And we embraced and kissed."

CIVIA GELBER BASCH was liberated at the Ravensbrück concentration camp in Germany, the largest Nazi camp built specifically for women, on April 30, 1945, the same day Adolf Hitler committed suicide in Berlin, some fifty miles away.

The Soviet forces that liberated the camp were greeted by more than 23,000 women, survivors of the approximately 115,000 inmates, most of them women and children, who had been murdered there over the previous two years. These inmates, from twenty-three nations, included political prisoners, Jehovah's Witnesses, and a large number of Rom, as well as Jews.

Civia was born on April 4, 1928, in Oradea Mare, in the region of Transylvania, in northwestern Romania. She was the youngest of fifteen children, five of whom died before she was born. The family lived in a large house, and there was a very large yard. They had a lumberyard, a flour mill, and an oil press. There was a great deal of farmland, and they raised chickens, ducks, geese, and turkeys. Her father, a Hasidic Jew, grew fruits and vegetables. "He could grow anything," she remembers. "Challenge to him was nothing."

Her early years were relatively tranquil. There were anti-Semitic laws and economic discrimination, but, Civia believes, "Romanian Jews had a good life. As anti-Semites go, you could buy the Romanians off and they could be your best friends until you turned your back." That changed drastically after August 1940, when Transylvania, where approximately 150,000 Jews lived, came under Hungarian rule. Soon after that Civia and her family were sent to a ghetto.

In 1942 her mother died, after which Civia was gradually separated from her family and her world. Her brothers were taken to the Ukrainian-Russian front and her sixteen-and-one-half-year-old sister died of pneumonia. Barely sixteen years old herself, she and her thirty-six-year-old sister (whom she had been visiting), together with hundreds of other Jews, were assembled in a courtyard and threatened with death if they did not give up all their valuables. Civia still recalls her anger at the sight of a Hasidic Jew squeezing a tube of toothpaste in which his jewelry had been hidden. The group was then herded into wagons for a two-day trip to the concentration camp in Auschwitz.

There Civia volunteered for work and was separated from her sister. After three months of hard labor she was moved to the camp at Ravensbrück. Understanding that a demonstration of her usefulness to the German cause would greatly improve her chances of survival, as it had at Auschwitz, the determined girl immediately volunteered for work once again. Some of the most powerful and respected German corporations

Female prisoners at forced labor dig trenches at the Ravensbrück concentration camp.
This photograph is from the SS-Propaganda-Album des Frauen-KZ-Ravensbrück 1940–1941.
Ravensbrück, Germany. 1940–1941.

employed concentration camp inmates as forced laborers (those who were not physically strong enough to survive were worked to death), and Civia was sent a few miles from the camp, to work for the Siemens Electrical Company, which manufactured airplanes and airplane parts for the Nazis.

Early in 1945 workers were ordered to start dismantling the Siemens factory, and prisoners were gradually transferred back to the main camp. They were given no reason, but Civia soon realized that something important was about to happen. Bombs could be heard falling on nearby Berlin, and she speculated that the Soviets were approaching. She remembers:

"The first inkling we had was when we took apart this factory. I was on a twenty-foot ladder, cutting wires. I said to my foreman—who was a civilian, a German civilian who was vicious, but he liked me—'What are we doing this for?' and he said something like, 'Let the next ones worry about it. . . .' So that was our very first inkling, and then the following weekend we got a . . . They had these five-pound Red Cross packages that had been sent to a warehouse but never given to the prisoners, and then all of a sudden the week before we were evacuated to the main camp, they gave, I think, one package for four prisoners, and that's when we found out that Roosevelt [U.S. President Franklin D. Roosevelt] had died, and we were so upset.

"That was the first time we had an idea, and then, after we had been evacuated—we had some Russian prisoners with us, prisoners of war, and there was a young woman doctor, I remember she must have been in her late twenties, and a German nurse who was a political prisoner, she was in her sixties. A couple of nights before the liberation, they were tearing sheets and they were talking about the Russians being close. . . . And then the next morning we got up and all the Germans were gone. The day before that they were shooting at each other, because they were blaming each other. They saw that the noose was on the neck. And then the next morning the gates were open. They had disappeared. And a Russian soldier on a bicycle came to liberate us, and the next time was a Russian soldier on a horse, and the next thing that we saw was a wagon full of bread, which, of course, everybody jumped on. And I think the Russian soldiers were as hungry as we were, because they really lived on very sparing rations. Lots of vodka. They drank everything, formaldehyde, you name it. Anything that had any kind of liquor in it . . ."

TONIA ROTKOPF BLAIR, born in Lodz, Poland, on September 18, 1925, was liberated while an inmate in the concentration camp at Mauthausen, Austria, in May 1945. Her family—she had an older sister and a younger brother—was a happy one. Though far from wealthy, they were comfortable, and the highest priority in the home was placed on education. They lived in a neighborhood that included Christians, but though they lived peacefully together, none of the non-Jews was numbered among their friends. It was that way throughout Poland. Anti-Semitism was taken for granted; there were Jews and there were Poles, but no Jewish Poles.

One week after the German invasion of Poland, Lodz, a busy industrial city, was occupied by the conquering army and annexed to Germany. Under the Nazi occupation, Jews had to observe early curfews and were not permitted to use streetcars or to walk on sidewalks. Tonia witnessed a terrifying and humiliating episode when her father, who had lost his job and had been forced to surrender his bankbook, was knocked down and brutally kicked by German soldiers. His crime:

Tonia's father, Mendel Rotkopf, and her mother, Miriam Gitla Rotkopf, on their wedding day. Lodz, Poland. 1921(?).

walking on the forbidden sidewalk. That, for the young girl, was "the beginning of the end."

But it was only the beginning.

In early February 1940 the Germans ordered the establishment of a ghetto. More than 150,000 Jews, more than a third of the population of the city, were forced to move into small apartments in a small, predominantly Jewish area. In early May the ghetto was formally closed. It was encircled with barbed wire, and guards had orders to kill any Jew (and, later, any Rom, since some five thousand of them were sent there from Austria and housed separately) who tried either to leave or to enter the area. Access to the ghetto was almost equally difficult for non-Jews, and as a consequence, food, which would have been brought in by non-Jews, was scarce, and starvation became common.

In time the Lodz ghetto became not just an area to which Jews were confined prior to deportation but an industrial center, where almost one hundred factories employed a large number of the Jewish residents as slave labor. Others were able to find nonfactory jobs. Among them was fourteen-year-old Tonia, who lied about her age in order to work as a

Tonia (far right), age 2½, and her family. From left to right: Cousin Bernard; Cousin Rozka; Cousin Regina; Cousin Tonia Plonski; Tonia Rotkopf's sister, Irena (standing); and Tonia's mother. All perished in the Holocaust except for the two Tonias. 1927.

nurse (it had long been her ambition to become one) in a foundling home. Since her workday ended later than the curfew imposed upon residents of the ghetto, Tonia slept at the foundling home most of the time and returned to her family's apartment only on her infrequent days off.

On one such occasion, carrying food she had managed to save at her job so that she might share it with her family, she found the entrance to the apartment sealed and the apartment itself empty. To her horror, she learned that her family had been among those many Jews who were periodically taken away in the middle of the night by the Nazis, destined for deportation and almost certain death. Having rushed to the area from which these victims usually left, she arrived just in time to see her family being marched away by heavily armed Nazi guards. It was the last time she saw her mother, father, sister, and brother.

The Lodz ghetto was liquidated in 1944. At that time some sixty-seven thousand of the sixty-eight thousand Jews still confined there were transferred to Auschwitz-Birkenau. Tonia, who had spent her last months in the ghetto working as a nurse in a Jewish hospital, was among them.

Tonia turned nineteen at the death camp. She has no memory of ever having eaten there—she never had a cup, bowl, or spoon—but she does recollect being so thirsty that, in desperation, she mistakenly drank from a bucket that contained a disinfectant.

Mercifully her stay at Auschwitz lasted only three weeks, after which she and a few hundred other girls were taken to an airplane factory–work camp at Freiberg, Germany. They remained there for several months, living in somewhat better conditions—only because the work she and the others were performing was of importance to the efforts of the German Army to delay its inevitable defeat at the hands of the approaching American and Soviet forces.

In the spring Tonia was again transferred, this time to another con-

The crematorium at Mauthausen. This photograph was taken by Tonia's friend Captain Ostich, who later went to fight in Japan. 1945.

centration camp, Mauthausen, where she and her good friend Bluma, a nurse she had met in the Lodz ghetto, arrived in April 1945 after a long journey through Czechoslovakia and into Austria.

Mauthausen, situated on a hilltop near Linz, had been established in 1938 to provide slave labor for the nearby granite quarries. It became known as one of the most brutal of concentration camps. Many prisoners were worked to death, others died of starvation or disease, and still others were killed when they were pushed from three-hundred-foot-high cliffs into the quarries. Jews were not the only prisoners at the camp. A large number of Rom, homosexuals, Jehovah's Witnesses, Polish Christians, Soviet prisoners of war, and tens of thousands of Spaniards, who had fought against fascism in their own country and had first been imprisoned in France, were among the interned. Mauthausen was liberated only a few weeks after Tonia's arrival, and she remembers her last days there:

"They took us down to wooden barracks, and we were all lying on the floor—not on wood or anything—and the floor was wet at night. I don't know how many days and nights, and there were really people dying there. Bluma was so sick that blood came out of her mouth, and many people could hardly lift their heads. They were lying on the floor, and I managed to crawl out—I was still strong enough. I was sitting in front of the barracks, against the door, and it was very sunny and warm. The barracks were on the bottom, and on the top of the mountain I saw a string of white cars with Red Cross on them. I don't know if I realized it myself or if it was someone else, but I crawled in and I thought I was screaming, 'Americans, the Americans, the Americans are here,' but I was obviously only whispering because Bluma said she couldn't hear anything, and other people lifted their heads just to hear the word *Americans*.

"I don't know what I felt when I realized we were free. No strength, I couldn't jump, I couldn't even walk, I could hardly stand up. I only know we wanted to be treated like human beings. We were chided later on, but we immediately wanted to have fresh sheets, clean sheets, and water to bathe. And we lost our appetites. I lost it completely. I couldn't eat, I just couldn't eat. After a while they gave me insulin to stimulate my appetite. . . . Right after liberation, the Americans gave us chocolate, which nobody could eat. And people were dying, and some people were strong enough and walked to town and they got potatoes, and they got dreadfully sick—one person died."

The American soldiers soon took over. They converted Nazi barracks into improvised hospitals for the survivors and fed them soft foods—cream of wheat and a light, rather watery but nourishing soup—in an effort to accustom them to a normal diet. Tonia, young and in relatively good health, responded to urgent calls for nurses and was given work by the Americans. Though she didn't understand English, she learned enough to get by. English was soon not necessary, as soldiers of the Soviet Army replaced the U.S. troops. The American withdrawal had been agreed upon by both armies—for strategic reasons—and the camp survivors were given a choice: to go with the Americans, as they were encouraged to do, or to wait behind for the Soviet occupiers. The vast majority chose to follow the Americans, but Tonia and Bluma, both starry-eyed young radicals, vigorously opposed to American capitalism, chose to wait for the Soviet occupiers.

AKIVA KOHANE was liberated on May 4, 1945, at Gunskirchen, a subcamp of Mauthausen.

Akiva's mother. Undated.

He was born on January 10, 1929, in the town of Katowice, in southern Poland, close to the German border. Just before the Germans invaded Poland, the Kohane family—Akiva, his younger sister, his father (a well-to-do importer of Swiss watches and clocks), and his mother—decided to move temporarily to Warsaw, to distance themselves from the border in case of a war, which they believed was imminent.

The move was of no avail. As expected, the invasion did take place, but the fighting continued for a longer time in Warsaw than in the rest of the country, and the Kohane family was forced to remain there for an extra four weeks. During that time their home in the capital was destroyed, but the family survived, and after the Germans arrived, they managed to get out and return to Katowice. But their hometown was unrecognizable. The Germans had been enthusiasti-

Akiva and his family at a summer mountain resort in Zakopane, Poland. Akiva is standing between his father and his uncle (far right). Akiva's father is holding his sister, who has ribbons in her hair. Akiva's mother is standing at the back. The other woman and child are distant family relatives. This is the only photograph Akiva has of his family. 1937(?).

cally welcomed, and Nazi flags and pictures of Hitler were everywhere.

Soon after their return to Katowice, an order was issued requiring all Jewish men to register prior to being sent away for approximately eight weeks of labor. Akiva's father was among those sent off. Instead of being away for eight weeks, however, he was gone for more than two years, during which time the Kohane marriage dissolved. Akiva's father never returned to their home. The family unit, so important in a time of crisis, was destroyed, and Akiva and his sister moved between one parent and the other, from town to town. In time Akiva's father disappeared, and Akiva learned several years later that he was last seen being deported from the Kraków ghetto.

Akiva and his mother and sister were forced to live as fugitives. They obtained false papers, identifying themselves as Christians, were sent to labor camps, where they bribed guards in order to escape, and ended up in the ghetto of Sosnowiec, not far from Kraków. In January 1944 the ghetto was destroyed, and they were taken the short distance to Auschwitz-Birkenau. There Akiva was separated from his mother and sister, whom he never saw again, and there he was examined by Dr. Josef Mengele (well known for his cruel medical experiments) and given a number, tattooed on his arm, to replace his name.

Akiva remained at Auschwitz until the middle of January 1945, when Soviet troops, as part of a surprise offensive, approached the area of the camp. Shortly after midnight on the night of the eighteenth the Nazis ordered a general evacuation. The prisoners were awakened and given the news. They were informed that they had a choice: If they wanted to remain, they could; if they wanted to leave, each would be given a whole loaf of bread and a piece of sausage as well as a blanket. Akiva knew what that meant. If you didn't go, it meant you were weak, and weak people, of no practical use to the Nazis, would be killed. Understanding this, he became one of approximately sixty thousand prisoners, mostly Jews, who were forced on a death march from Auschwitz to Wodzisław, in the western part of Upper Silesia. Some fifteen thousand prisoners died during this march.

Upon their arrival at Wodzisław, Akiva was put on a cattle train and transported to Mauthausen. "Auschwitz," Akiva remembers, "was like a country club, in comparison to what happened in Mauthausen."

The largest concentration camp in Austria, Mauthausen grew enormously in early 1945 as the result of a great influx of Hungarian Jews—part of the Nazis' last-minute scheme to eliminate the entire Hungarian Jewish population—as well as of a large number of prisoners transferred there from other camps. With the overcrowding, conditions became increasingly perilous for the inmates, and many died from starvation or disease. During his stay in Mauthausen, Akiva was housed in a tent camp that had been hastily built to accommodate the new arrivals. But his stay was short. The frontiers of the war were approaching, with Allied forces advancing from the east and from the west, and the Germans were desperately moving prisoners from one camp to another, apparently in a senseless effort to hide at least some of their crimes from the rest of the world. As a result, Akiva and a group of prisoners embarked on a second death march, this time to Gunskirchen.

Conditions were no better there, with prisoners crammed into log structures or tar paper sheds. Akiva recollects:

> "We had to sit on the floor, and one person was sitting inside the other. Now if you have to go out, everybody has to get up and let you out. When you come back you don't find your place anymore. And the worst part is that when we arrived in that camp after three days' march from Mauthausen, it started to rain. You could be sleeping outside because it was a nice forest, but it was constantly raining. So we had to squeeze inside that camp. . . ."

At the end of April there was an unexplained change. Somehow, the International Red Cross had learned of conditions in the camp and sent representatives there from its headquarters in Geneva, Switzerland.

> "They brought some food for us, half of which was taken by the SS themselves, because they were hungry, too. Not like us, but all of a sudden they got the good stuff from Geneva, chocolate and meat. And then they started to distribute it to us. So first they called women and children. Then people started to push, of course, so when they started to push they took out guns, and they started to shoot. They were playing games with that food. The official food that they were giving us from the camp was kind of a soup which was basically kind of a sweet water. And we found out later that this was poisoned. We noticed all of a sudden that people started to die more quickly than before.

People were just falling like flies, but we didn't know from what. We would have eaten the soup for another few days, nobody would have survived."

Only a few days later their ordeal came to an end. For many of the prisoners, including Akiva, it was at first impossible to understand that they were liberated.

"On May 4th, it was a Friday, all of a sudden it was not raining that day so we were walking around the forest, and all of a sudden somebody came and said he didn't see any more of the guards around us. It was hard to see anyway because this was a forest, not like a regular camp that you see towers in front. But they didn't see anybody. And then we heard a few shots and the rumor started to spread that that's it, that the SS ran away. And then somebody told me that he saw a soldier—he didn't know if he was Russian or American, because it could be either one since this was actually not far from where the Russians and Americans came together. I don't remember any special jumping for joy or things like that. People were in such a situation that they really couldn't care less. I mean, when I say that now it sounds funny. But you know we were one-half dead, so the only thing that I was happy about the night that followed was that I didn't have to go back to the barracks, that I could sleep outside. I stayed with a friend of mine I knew from Auschwitz, a Dutch guy. Some people started to leave right away, to go out. As it was getting dark, I didn't know where to go. I preferred to go to sleep without being squeezed in the barrack.

"The following day the Dutch guy and I started to walk towards the road, and then something happened to me. I saw all those people that had died or were dying, and here we were liberated. This was the worst part, that we were finally liberated, and if they could have held on for another few days they, too, would be liberated, but they had to die.

"I walked out from that forest to the highway, and all of a sudden something occurred to me. Where should I go? It was the first time in my life that I was by myself, and I didn't know. When I was a child, I was with my parents, and they were telling me where to go or what to do. When I was in the camp, the Germans used to tell me what to do. Now I had to make the decision myself.

"Well, when I went out on the road, I didn't know should I go left or right? There was an American MP, who was directing traffic; there was still fighting on the left side so we could only go to the right. He was directing to the right, so I just followed everybody else."

The American soldiers who liberated the camp were unprepared for the horrors they faced. They had been trained to fight and to win military battles, not to witness, organize, and give solace and help to these newly freed prisoners. In Akiva's words, the prisoners were "zombies running around like animals." Even now, more than a half century later, most of these soldiers prefer not to talk about what they found in and around Gunskirchen, and when they do, they speak of the inmates as "skinny and bony," of taut, waxen skin drawn over skulls, elbows, and knees, and of human feces everywhere, as well as of the unbearable stench. "All were in rags which hung on their frames in odd arrangements, patched, bulky, tattered, ill-fitting," one young American rifleman has been quoted as saying, "but then how could one outfit a scarecrow?"

Initially, well-intentioned American soldiers, passing by in army trucks, showered these newly freed prisoners with food, not realizing that a normal diet could be dangerous and even fatal to them. Many of the former prisoners, too, failed to realize the perils of overeating after months and even years of near starvation. Akiva's experience immediately following liberation parallels that of many others:

"We were walking, walking, and eventually we got to a place where they had a lot of food. They discovered that not far from our camp there was a huge place where food was stored. So, of course, we broke in there—there was no law, everybody was doing whatever he wanted. And we just broke in. I will never forget this. I saw one guy who got a huge can of beef, and he finished the whole can. And he dropped dead still holding the can in his hand. The stomach couldn't take it. And people were running all over, going to the neighboring population and just walking in and robbing anything they could and getting anything, mainly food. . . ."

After the Liberation: The Search

It is not possible to picture this chaotic Europe where thousands of people were on the march from "nowhere to nowhere," searching for a place to live, searching for homes that did not exist, searching for husbands or wives, searching for children. Waves of homeless human beings were rolling all over Europe, not only Jews but former underground workers, political prisoners, human beings of almost all European nationalities.

—Gabriele D. Schiff

Previous page: View of the destruction on the site of the Warsaw ghetto. Warsaw, Poland. 1945.

Jewish survivors who had been set free in postwar Europe had experienced years of indescribable suffering. Under normal circumstances, they would have celebrated their freedom by eagerly returning to their homes and families, in order to regain their strength and resume their lives. These had not been normal circumstances, however, and they soon realized that it would not be possible to pick up where they had left off. Profoundly damaged themselves, both physically and emotionally, they soon learned that they had lost all or almost all their relatives and close friends as well as their homes and properties. Their towns and villages had become mass graveyards; their community life and their rich culture had been obliterated. Everything in their cities and towns and villages would remind them of years of humiliation, of unthinkable atrocities, of tragedy and irreparable loss.

For these reasons, few survivors attempted to return to their homes, and most of those who did stayed only a short time. It would be impossible, they soon understood, for them to live in places so closely linked to their childhoods, and it would be impossible to build new lives and new homes on these ruins.

Other factors influenced the majority of European Jews in their decisions not to return to their homes. Although some non-Jews in Nazi-occupied lands had risked their own lives to save the lives of their Jewish neighbors, most of them had actively cooperated with the Nazis. As a result, the Jews who returned home would find themselves living side by side with many of the people who had aided in the mass destruction of their fellow Jews.

These non-Jews, it became clear, had not changed their ways. Anti-Semitism had not diminished. On the contrary, as soon as the war came to an end, word spread that the Jews who did return to their homes were

Postwar demonstration of Polish Jews against Fascism. The demonstrators carry a Yiddish banner reading, "Honor for the fallen martyrs killed by the Fascist murderers." Lodz, Poland. 1945.

for the most part welcomed not with compassion and apologies but with anger. Their former neighbors all too frequently blamed them for the outbreak of the war and lamented the fact that the Germans had not done a thorough job of eliminating them.

Although many returning Jews were greeted with hostility throughout much of Europe, the situation in Poland, where some fifty thousand Jews survived out of a prewar population of more than three million, was especially tragic. The roots of anti-Semitism were deeply embedded in Poland. After the war, Jews who went home were attacked and beaten and sometimes warned that they would be killed if they did not leave the country by a specified date. They had good reason to fear for their lives: It has been estimated that 363 Jews were murdered in liberated Poland in 1945. Pogroms, organized massacres of Jews, spread like an epidemic throughout the country. Overwhelmed by fear of betraying their identity, Jews were afraid to speak Yiddish in public, and those with beards were afraid to walk down the street. Many Jews who had saved themselves during the German occupation by carrying false Christian documents felt it necessary to continue to use the same documents after the war.

Most dramatically, on July 4, 1946, forty-two Jewish survivors in the town of Kielce were shot, stoned, slashed with axes, and otherwise murdered. They had been accused of abducting Christian children for ritual purposes. It was an ages-old, viciously anti-Semitic, and absurd accusation. Clearly, even after millions of Jews had perished during the Nazi occupation, the Polish masses were still consumed with hatred, and many were determined to complete the job that Hitler had failed to accomplish: the total extermination of the Jewish people.

Word of the bloody massacre at Kielce spread throughout Poland, and as a result, thousands of Jews who had hoped to remain fled the country. The Polish Jews had reached the same conclusion that was reached by the majority of survivors who had tried to return home not only in Poland but throughout Europe.

A German woman views a bombed-out storefront in Munich, one year after the end of the war. Munich, Germany. April–May 1946.

ANN SHORE was among those who tried. Following their liberation by the Russians in January 1945, Ann, her mother, and her sister were warned to wait awhile before leaving their hiding place. Returning Jews, they were told, were being murdered without provocation in Zabno, their hometown. When, after a few days, they did return, life proved to be so dangerous that they remained for only a few weeks. Ann was not surprised.

"I was born into anti-Semitism. We were Jews—an isolated group with a common enemy. Polish people hated Jews—it was a given. No one has an answer why. When you are a child, you know you are simply part of a group of people who have an enemy. It could be a next-door neighbor. You have no control at all. You're scared of that person. I was born into a culture where we knew that Jews were hated.

"We stayed in our town for five weeks, hoping and waiting for people to return. Only a few others came back from their hiding places. Seven hundred Jews from our town perished. Not a single person returned from the concentration camps. Rumors had it that they had all been gassed. In our town only fifteen Jews survived. Our vibrant Jewish community had disappeared as if it never existed. My uncles, aunts, my cousins, and my two grandmothers that I loved so much had perished. I would never again see my little friends. They had all vanished in the crematoriums. My world was shattered."

It would be too painful for Ann and her family to attempt to remain in Zabno, and there was no reason for them to do so.

ALICIA WEINSBERG saw no reason to remain in Warsaw, the city of her birth, following liberation. After escaping from the ghetto, Alicia had been hidden in and around the capital during the German occupation and had returned to an apartment there following the war. But she and her family, informed of the fate of Jews throughout the country, could never again feel at home in Warsaw, and soon the sixteen-year-old girl was able to persuade her parents that life would always be dangerous for the Jews of Poland. They should, she believed, make every effort to leave the country and settle elsewhere.

AKIVA KOHANE reached the same conclusion without even trying to resume life in Poland. When, at a temporary refugee camp in the American sector of Germany, he was asked where he wanted to go, he was certain of only one thing: He did not want to be repatriated to Poland. He no longer had family or friends there; they had all been killed, and he had no desire to spend his life among the Polish people.

LARRY ROSENBACH also showed no interest in resettling in Poland, where he no longer had a family or a home or any emotional ties, but merely painful memories of his childhood and the years spent in work and concentration camps.

TONIA BLAIR, however, did return to Lodz. The Soviets had maintained their postwar role as occupier of Mauthausen for only a short time. Their main concern was to facilitate the return of the freed prisoners to their countries of origin. For this reason—the survivors were given no choice—Tonia and her friend Bluma left the camp after a few months. They traveled by truck to Vienna, where they were put on a train for the one-day journey home. They were very well treated by their Soviet escorts during the trip and were given plenty of food—bread and fruit and sausages—but their welcome upon their arrival in Lodz was terrifying.

"We arrive at the train station, and we don't know what to

do. We get off the train, and there's the platform, and I lean against the wall. For some reason I was separated from my group, and a few Poles come up and say, 'Look at them, they still survived. We thought they killed them off.' I got so scared, and my knees turned; I didn't say anything because very often they told me I don't look Jewish—whatever Jewish-looking is. I could have had the Russian soldiers arrest those people. . . . But all of a sudden men not from our group came, and they took us away. There was already a Jewish organization, and they took us there. I don't remember much of it, but then we were alone in a giant apartment somewhere. I was the youngest, and Bluma became my mentor.

"We didn't even go out much at all—we were just in this apartment . . . and then we were planning to leave. They said we can't stay here—I don't know why not—but I didn't realize what was going on, that they were plotting to leave Poland and go to the American zone. The atmosphere must have been so terrible that I only realize now that we didn't venture out. We didn't even go on the main street. . . . In Poland it was Poles versus Jews. I only remember darkness.

"You're finally home, but you don't have a home. My home—I didn't even go there—was occupied by Polish people. That's one of the things I understand from what I read: Some Jews had their homes taken and wanted their homes back. My family had only a little one-room apartment, but some people had homes—that's why they were afraid. That's why there was a terrible pogrom at Kielce. People wanted to kill us again because they had thought we were gone.

"It was a strange land in a way. I had pored over—I don't know where I did that, maybe at some Jewish organization—over books and books of names to find family or extended family, but I didn't find anybody. Bluma, however, had found a cousin, a man who had been liberated earlier by the Russians. Bluma, this cousin, his wife, and myself were planning to go to the American zone. I didn't know it then, but I soon learned that the Poles would not allow Polish citizens to leave the country. So it was decided that our whole group couldn't leave together— just a few at a time. Among those who were permitted to leave Poland were the *Volksdeutsche*—Germans who had been sent to occupy Poland during the war and wanted to return to Germany after it—and when the four of us reached the train station to catch a train for Berlin, the station was full of those returning Germans. I've never seen an uglier crowd in my life—screaming, fighting, arguing. . . . I said, 'This is the master race, right, the master race?' Anyway, we pretended we were part of them, so we were able to leave Lodz and get on the train to Berlin."

GEORGE SCHWAB never even thought of going back to his home in Latvia. Soon after his liberation he was taken to a German military hospital, run by the British, where he spent weeks regaining his strength. While there, he was visited by a number of Russian officers, who were accompanied by British officers.

"The Russians were anxious to get those who were born in the East back to Russia, to Latvia. I was promised all sorts of wonderful things, going back to the fatherland, so on and so forth. But, as a twelve-year-old boy in 1944, aboard a Nazi troopship packed with Jews as it left Riga for Danzig, I had taken a vow: 'Never, but never will I return to this blood-soaked country called Latvia.' We had made a contract among the members of the family, never to go back East. And I was told by my mother, when it all started, never to go back to Latvia. 'To survive, go West. Never go back, go forward.' However much the Soviet officers and British officers tried to convince me to go back, I said no. Even though I was very young I could not be persuaded. I absolutely refused. Many of my friends with whom I had spent the war years did choose to go back, and many were first taken not to Latvia but to Siberia. In the sixties and seventies they were permitted to come back to Latvia. Many of those who survived are now in Israel and very much regret the decision they had made. And I always think back how close I was to ending up where they ended up. But I was stubborn. . . ."

JUDITH BIHALY was in Budapest, the city of her birth, when the war ended for her, and the distance to her home in miles was not very great. But she was alone—without family or friends—and, still a young child, she was frightened and understood little of where she had been or even where she was. Lost and confused at the time, she remembers that she was one of a number of children who, following liberation, had been put onto a wagon and taken to some kind of Jewish institution. She recalls her return home:

"I was sleeping on a shelf of bunks, just high enough for me to shimmy onto. I remember someone yelling into my face, asking, 'Why don't you answer?' The person called me by name, and I imagine she must have been calling me for some time, because she was angry with me. I remember being very scared and shocked because I didn't want anyone to know that I existed. I was very upset that somebody actually knew my name. It felt as if someone cruelly called me back from wherever I was.

"This person said, 'You have to go to the office.' So I went to the office, and they asked me why I was still there. I didn't know, and they said, 'Well, why don't you go home?'

"So I said, 'I don't know where I am.' I don't remember the name of the place they told me, but it was in Budapest. They said, 'You have to go home now.' I said, 'Yes, but I don't know how to get home.' They said, 'Well, you know your address?' I said I did and gave them my address.

"They said, 'Well, you go out on the street and you ask for directions, and you'll get home.'

"I remember being so scared, so frightened. I don't remember how I found my home, but I do remember ringing my doorbell and hearing a dog barking. Somebody opened the door, and I said my name. The person who answered the door wasn't yelling or anything, but I could tell that he or she was very angry and said, 'If you don't get away from here right away, I'm going to let the dog loose on you.'

"So, without a word, I just turned away."

CIVIA BASCH also returned to the city of her birth, in hopes of resettling there after the war, but she, too, found it impossible to do so. Her ties with her home and with Romania had been severed.

Following liberation, the Soviets had begun to establish a kind of order in Ravensbrück. They transferred the sick and disabled former prisoners to a hospital that had been set up on the site of the Siemens factory, where Civia had worked. Civia remained in the hospital for three months, after which she was given permission to travel back to her home.

Civia began the long journey across Europe, from Ravensbrück to Berlin and then through Czechoslovakia and Hungary to Romania. The first night was spent in a railroad station in the town of Ravensbrück, where Civia and a number of other refugees awaited a train for Berlin. They were hoping to make contact with a Jewish organization that could help them reach their destinations. Threatened and chased that entire night by their drunken Soviet liberators (who had been long deprived of any contact with women), she remembers this as

> "probably the scariest night, next to being next to the gas chambers, that we experienced. . . . And all this time we were waiting for daylight. And we were so petrified. Imagine, now you're liberated by your liberators and they're trying to . . . but I guess it was all the years that they spent in the war. I have no idea, but they were really barbaric about it."

The following morning Civia managed to escape and make her own way to Berlin, and from there she traveled to Oradea Mare, her family's home in Romania.

> "I went back to my hometown, and I looked around. The house was totally empty, but I sort of set up housekeeping. The only thing that waited for me was my little gray cat, who must have been visiting the house all the time, I don't know. As soon as I got to the door, I felt something around my legs, and there was a little cat; we had cats and dogs because we had a big yard.
>
> "I couldn't believe that my father hadn't come home. And I don't even know when he died, or how, but they told me that once they shaved his beard off, because he was Hasidic, he wouldn't eat. He stopped eating. He was so destroyed when my mother died, and one thing after another . . . and then this tragedy came.
>
> "In any case, after six months I had nothing in the house, so our next-door neighbor, who was my teacher, whose daughters lived in our house most of the time—they were very well-to-do people—she had things of ours in every room, as did everyone

else, so she did me a favor. She gave me a blanket, a towel, some homespun sheets, a pillow, I think, and I stuck around for a while. But then I saw that things were changing there. It was Romania, but it wasn't the same. And it wasn't only that. Everywhere I went there was our stuff. There were people there living off of my father. Somebody walked down the street with my brother's suit on. I walked into somebody's house, and the curtains were ours. 'No, they're not yours; I know, my sister made them. . . .' "

There was no reason for Civia, not yet eighteen years old, to stay in Romania. Romania's Jewish community had been decimated. Once one of the most vital in Europe, the Jewish population had dwindled to fewer than three hundred thousand, from the more than eight hundred thousand who had lived there before the Holocaust. No longer attached to her homeland or welcomed there, Civia accepted the offer of two men who asked her to join a group of young people on their way to Palestine.

Polish Jewish DPs arrive in the American zone of Berlin after being smuggled by Bricah over the border from the Russian sector. Berlin, Germany. January 24, 1946.

The DP Camps

Anybody you met said, "Where were you? Who were you? Did you know so-and-so?"

—Tonia Blair

All who work with Hitler's victims really deal with people who have hidden scars, much more difficult to detect, often more difficult to deal with or alleviate than open wounds.

—Gabriele D. Schiff

I wanted to take everything in. In addition to studying English, Latin, German, geometry, geography, math, and literature, I took piano lessons. . . . Then I took horseback riding and dancing. . . . These were the most happy times for me. Everything was so exciting. I loved being with people, loved dancing, talking, I loved life.

—Ann Shore

Previous page: The entrance to the Finkenschlag DP camp.
Fürth, Germany. 1946–1947.

An estimated seven to nine million Europeans were exiled or displaced by the Second World War. The Jewish survivors of the Holocaust were among these, but they were a small percentage of all displaced persons, or DPs, as they became known. Others included the Rom, homosexuals, and physically or mentally disabled people who had miraculously escaped death at the hands of the Nazis; former slave laborers who had been brought to work in Germany's farms and factories; former prisoners of war; and countless other uprooted Europeans, who had either emigrated voluntarily to help the German war effort in the early 1940s or had fled from their homes as the Soviet armies advanced in 1944. The displaced persons camps were a short-term solution for many refugees who were on their way home, or who showed no desire to return to their countries of origin, or who were unwilling or unable to remain in their homes once they did return.

The plight of the DPs had been foreseen as early as 1943, when, under the leadership of the United States, the United Nations Relief and Rehabilitation Administration (UNRRA) was established. The organization's goal was to provide services for postwar refugees and, above all, to facilitate the repatriation of the anticipated flood of men, women, and children uprooted by the war.

As a consequence, in 1945, following Germany's surrender, UNRRA was already in place and able to play a large role in organizing the homeward journey of the great majority of the refugees. It was a daunting task, but because of these early preparations, nearly all the DPs were repatriated and resettled within little more than a year.

Very few Jewish DPs, however, were among the returnees. Because there was no Jewish state, no country the Jews could call their own, and no country that would welcome the Jews with wholehearted enthusiasm,

Jewish displaced persons eat in the main dining hall at the Landsberg DP camp. Landsberg, Germany. December 6, 1945.

their situation was different and the solutions were far more complex.

UNRRA was called upon to establish and supervise a number of transit camps for the remaining DPs (not all of them Jewish) in three of the four zones of occupation into which Germany and Austria had been divided after the war: the American, British, and French. The Soviets, who controlled the fourth zone, did not seem to be concerned with the problem. The transit camps were meant to be places of temporary refuge in which displaced persons could live while recovering physically and emotionally from their ordeals, decide what course their lives might take, and wait to be granted asylum by countries in which they hoped to be able to begin their new lives.

From the very beginning, the organizers and administrators of these camps experienced enormous difficulties. Many of these difficulties can be attributed to the lack of professional training of the UNRRA workers, who arrived completely unprepared for their jobs, as well as incompetence and lack of understanding on the part of the inexperienced American soldiers, who shared responsibilities with the UNRRA workers in the camps of the U.S. zone. It was reported that some soldiers, though well meaning, knew so little about the situation that they naively asked concentration camp survivors what crimes they had committed to warrant such cruel punishments. Many difficulties, on the other hand, were inevitable, given the cicumstances under which these facilities were prepared: hurriedly, and in the middle of a continent that had only just emerged from the chaos and destruction of a long and costly war.

Medical and sanitary facilities were poor, and food supplies limited, in both quality and quantity. Living quarters for the DPs were often inadequate. Men, women, and children were housed in military bases, former prisoner of war camps, abandoned training areas, decrepit schoolhouses, and barns. Even former concentration camps were hastily converted into assembly centers. The use of every available space is understandable under the circumstances, but it is hard to excuse the fact that because of a clothing shortage, many of the former prisoners were initially forced to wear their concentration camp uniforms and were sometimes housed with their former enemies. Many of the Holocaust survivors found themselves once again surrounded by barbed wire fences, living next to their former guards in overcrowded, filthy, inhumane camps, where they were all too often subject to humiliating treatment and anti-Semitic attacks.

During their first months in the transit camps, the destitute men and women were depressed and demoralized. At first they were too weary and dazed to air their complaints effectively, but soon word of the conditions under which they were living reached officials in Washington, D.C. The U.S. government moved swiftly. In July 1945 Henry Morgenthau, the secretary of the treasury, with the endorsement and encouragement of President Harry S. Truman, appointed Earl Harrison, dean of the law school of the University of Pennsylvania and a former commissioner of immigration, to head a delegation to investigate conditions in the DP camps in the U.S. zone of Germany. The group visited more than thirty camps, and its report, issued in the summer of 1945, was devastating in its condemnation of the conditions it found. The following were among the proposed reforms:

Jews should be recognized as a separate group and should not be forced to share housing with non-Jewish DPs, many of whom were known to be Nazis and anti-Semites. (According to the policy up to that time, groups were to be housed solely by nationality.)

Jews should be given the greatest degree of autonomy possible—and as quickly as possible.

Jewish residents should be allowed to live outside the camps, and German properties were to be set aside for their use if necessary.

Far greater efforts had to be made to help the DPs reunite with their families and look for lost friends and relatives. (Up to this point DPs were unable to do this themselves since they had not been allowed to send or receive mail.)

Convinced that the only long-term solution to the refugee problem was the emigration of the Jews to Palestine, Harrison recommended that the British be asked to issue a hundred thousand entry permits at once—without waiting for an overall settlement of the Palestine question, which concerned an eventual division of the land there between Jews and Arabs. The Jewish DPs, Harrison urged, should receive "the first and not the last attention," and he asked that the United States, too,

EMIGRATION TO PALESTINE

Many European Jews had, since the turn of the last century and the emergence of the Zionist movement, dreamed of establishing a state of their own in Palestine, a Middle Eastern land between the Mediterranean Sea and the Jordan River. In 1920 the League of Nations had given Great Britain a mandate to govern the territory, at the time inhabited by both Jews and Arabs. The British at first supported the idea of a Jewish state, but under pressure from the oil-rich Arab countries, which were alarmed by the enormous increase in Jewish immigration following the war, they withdrew their support. More than that, they actively opposed Jewish immigration to Palestine, allowing only 13,100 refugees to enter legally in 1945. In spite of this, Jewish refugees found ways of reaching Palestine by sea.

Beginning in August 1946, the British attempted to halt this immigration by capturing and deporting would-be immigrants to the island of Cyprus, where more than 50,000 refugees were held in detention camps.

On November 29, 1947, the United Nations General Assembly voted to partition Palestine into two separate states, Arab and Jewish. Early in April 1948 the British began to withdraw their forces from the area, ending their mandate, and on May 14 the establishment of the independent State of Israel was declared. The U.S. government immediately recognized the new Jewish state, and countries around the world soon followed its lead.

Having achieved their goal—the creation of a state of their own—the Jewish immigrants from Europe (as well as those who had already settled there) faced new and difficult trials. Immediately after the establishment of the State of Israel, the country was invaded by five of its Arab neighbors, an invasion that was successfully repulsed by the newly created Israeli Army. Peacetime challenges followed: Cities and villages had to be built, crops had to be planted, and a population from all over the world had to be integrated into one nation. In spite of many difficulties, the State of Israel flourished in the years after its establishment. Between 1948 and 1951, approximately seven hundred thousand Jews—two-thirds of them displaced persons from Europe—traveled to their new homeland, and since that time Jewish immigration to Israel has been unrestricted.

accept a larger number of the DPs. In an indignant conclusion, he wrote: "We appear to be treating the Jews as the Nazis treated them, except that we do not exterminate them. They are in concentration camps in large numbers under our military guard instead of S.S. troops. One is led to wonder if the German people, seeing this, are not supposing that we are following or at least condoning Nazi policy."

After carefully studying Harrison's report, President Truman sent it on to General Dwight D. Eisenhower, drawing his attention to the passage cited above and urging the general to look into the matter personally. In September 1945 Eisenhower inspected five of the camps, two of them exclusively Jewish and a third one largely so. After the visit, he wrote to the president expressing his agreement on the seriousness of the situation and offering a sympathetic and perceptive analysis of the problems facing the Jewish DPs. He also assured Truman that conditions at the camps had improved considerably since the time of the Harrison report—to a great extent because of efforts made by the U.S. Army. "I am confident that if you could compare conditions now with what they were three months ago, you would realize that your Army here has done an admirable and almost unbelievable job in this respect," he concluded.

Eisenhower's appraisal of the situation was a fair one. Many of Harrison's recommendations had already been implemented, and conditions at the camps had improved by the time the general arrived, though no action had been taken concerning Harrison's plea that Great Britain and the United States allow the emigration of more of the refugees. (Truman did, at the end of 1945, grant preferential treatment to DPs who wanted to come to the United States).

Even greater and more significant changes were to follow, as it became clear by the end of 1945 that the camps would have to be transformed from transit camps, where the survivors would spend short periods of time, to self-sustaining communities, where the refugees would have to wait for many months and even years before being able to make arrangements to move on to other countries.

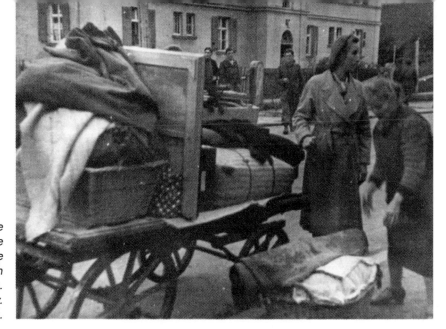

German women are forced to evacuate their homes to make room for Jewish displaced persons. Landsberg, Germany. January 1, 1946.

The main reason for this was the tremendous and unexpected increase in the population of the camps. Instead of the anticipated decrease following the resettlement of the refugees, the camps grew as a new wave of Jewish refugees began to arrive after having fled Eastern Europe and its brand of Soviet anti-Semitism. Furthermore, the survivors were not moving on as quickly as predicted, either because they were physically or emotionally incapable of doing so or because they simply were not welcome elsewhere.

Most of the Jewish DPs, refusing repatriation, chose to emigrate to Palestine, but the British were doing their best to deny access to all but a limited number of Jewish settlers. Many other DPs wanted to resettle in the United States, where relatives or friends lived, but were rebuffed because of rigid immigration restrictions, which prevented the admission of more than a few thousand refugees per year.

As a consequence, the estimated number of Jewish DPs still seeking new homes reached 250,000 in 1946: 185,000 in Germany, 45,000 in Austria, and 20,000 in Italy. Profoundly damaged by the Holocaust, they remained outcasts even after those years had come to an end.

The complex task of making what could be a long waiting period useful meant providing an environment in which DPs could be successfully rehabilitated and better equipped to function on their own, both socially and professionally, in lands that would be foreign to them. Not only would camp living conditions and medical facilities have to be improved, but educational programs for children and young people and vocational training programs for adults would have to be established and administered. In time there would have to be schools and small factories or workshops. All this meant equipment: tools and machines as well as textbooks, notebooks, blackboards, and chalk. Recreational centers, too, would be important as places for dancing and singing and athletic activities.

Most of all, it was essential that there be skilled and compassionate personnel who not only could function as administrators but also provide individual DPs with both psychological guidance and practical help, including advice concerning their plans for emigration.

Fortunately, following the Harrison Report, which sanctioned and encouraged the use of professionally trained representatives from a number of American welfare agencies, such dedicated workers were made available to the camps. The U.S. Army continued to control the camps themselves, and the DPs were supplied with the basic necessities of life by UNRRA until 1947, when the International Refugee Organization assumed UNRRA's duties. But as a result of an agreement between UNRRA and the army, an increasingly large share of the responsibility for tending to the needs of the refugees was delegated to members of the American Jewish Joint Distribution Committee, known as the Joint. This private social welfare organization, based in the United States, financed many of the vocational and educational activities in the U.S. zone, helped feed and clothe many thousands of the DPs, and generously contributed to the cost of emigration when necessary. The Organization for Rehabilitation through Training (ORT) was largely responsible for occupational training.

One of the representatives of the Joint was Gabriele D. Schiff, a senior social worker who began working in the DP camps in late 1946 and remained there until 1949. She remembers:

"People were thin, they were ill, and they were bitter. If this was 'liberation,' why survive? People had kept themselves alive, barely so, in the concentration camps, with the hope of going to America or Palestine. But neither the Americans nor the British in Palestine said, 'Welcome.'

"And so the endless waiting for clearance and papers began: the hopeless battle with bureaucracy. This in itself was almost insurmountable, as was working in defeated countries without sufficient housing and food or a working economy. There was a British zone, an American zone, and a French zone; all had different administrations. All they had in common was a mass of desperate, demanding, ever shifting humanity, who felt, and perhaps rightly so, that having suffered so much to survive, the world owed them a living. . . ."

The bitterness that Mrs. Schiff noted was confirmed by the testimonies of many of the survivors. One, Samuel Bak, an artist, wrote:

"In some ways, we were a disturbing and uncomfortable 'merchandise' that was trying to sell itself and longed to be acquired. The DP camp was supposed to be a place for brief stays only, but the world did not want us, and so we had nowhere to go. We often felt like we were some rare species in a zoo, visited by well-meaning but ineffectual observers who came from distant places of opportunity and freedom. Many of the visitors were very decent and devoted American Jews who observed our plight with pained hearts. . . . Meanwhile, we were condemned to wait and to wait and to wait. The hoped-for Jewish State was not for tomorrow, 'but maybe the day after.' "[1]

The DPs had many complaints, most of them justified and all of them easy to understand, given their troubled histories and the anxieties, doubts, and conflicts that clouded their futures. They were impatient and angry at having to line up for clothing or for showers or for inoculation against disease. They were forced to endure DDT spraying or steam baths—painful reminders of the concentration camps.

Mrs. Schiff has written:

"What many of us as workers had to learn and to accept was that to survive being in a concentration camp, in hiding, in any form of survival, people had to develop a different form of ethics which was not always acceptable in a so-called free society. Much aggression blew off in the constant battle about food. It was not enough, it was not cooked right, it was not kosher, it was too kosher. But mostly, it was not enough, because people wanted it to appease quite different needs."[2]

Akiva Kohane remembers his experience in a DP camp and offers his own analysis of it. He agrees that food itself was not really the issue. It is instead likely that the complaints and protests grew from the mere existence of any restriction as well as frustration at what seemed to the DPs to be the slow pace of their complete return to a normal world.

"I remember complaining that what they did give us—whoever was supplying the food—was not adequate. Because they gave us only a certain amount of bread. Maybe it was psychological. You know, if they said, 'Here is the bread, eat as much as you can,' we would probably have taken one piece and that's it. But because you knew it was somehow rationed, to a certain extent, we were always complaining about things like that."

Given the prevailing conditions, Mrs. Schiff has written, the organizations responsible for the camps did a "superhuman" job.

"But they did not earn much thanks. The displaced persons had three alternate ways to relate to authority—to distrust it, to out-maneuver it, or to try to ingratiate themselves with those in power. There was an all-prevailing fear of anyone in uniform. One did not have the courage to trust even one's friends. People had survived by maneuvering or by any method that could keep them alive, not only from day to day but literally hour to hour. It was a daily struggle to help people in a German camp, surrounded by former enemies, feeling discriminated against by the Allies, feeling forgotten by fate, and doing everything possible to make their voices heard. . . . They used the waiting period to find new life partners; marriages were rushed and so were babies. There was an all-consuming desire and obligation felt by the remnants of European Jewry, an almost holy commitment that the Jewish people must continue.

"At the risk of destroying a well-known cliché, I affirm that suffering does not make people any better; it often brings out the worst in them. At times all of us who worked in the camps were bitterly discouraged. We did our best to make living conditions bearable, but living in a camp, year after year, after having survived Hitler, is simply not human. Our clients could not understand that we ourselves were helpless in making bureaucracy move faster. . . . I think what united us was the one wish— to see the camp dissolved and to see the day when thousands of homeless people would be given a chance to build a home again. . . ."[2]

The first photo taken of Ann after her time in hiding. Berlin, Germany. 1946.

ANN SHORE did not reach a DP camp until the winter of 1946, more than a year after her liberation. During that period she demonstrated extraordinary resilience in regaining both her physical strength and her remarkable zest for living.

Unable to remain in Zabno, where their community had disappeared and their lives were endangered, Ann and her family had traveled to Tarnów, a larger city some ten miles away, where they were given shelter at an old hotel that was being used as a temporary home for returning refugees. It was a place where the homeless survivors could stay while deciding what path they should follow on the road back to life; a place where they could await—most often in vain—the return of friends and relatives. Shortly after their arrival in Tarnów, Ann's mother and sister, both in weakened condition from their years in hiding, were admitted to a hospital, where they stayed for two months. Ann, on her own, began to resume her life. She remembers:

"The place we stayed was on Goldhamera Street. We were being helped by some Jewish organizations and were given food and rooms—usually places to share with others. . . . Everything was fine. I didn't care where they put me, because I had experienced everything, and it's all secondary. As long as we had no more fear of death, everything was terrific. It was much safer for us to be there; there were many more Holocaust survivors living there, and we also had security. I remember people returning from the concentration camps, from Russia, and hiding places. I remember a little boy showing us the concentration camp number tattooed on his arm. Everyone was waiting and hoping that a family member would return. Daily they looked at lists, hoping to find the names of their loved ones. Every day new people would arrive. There was so much talk, so much sadness, everyone had a horrific story to tell. Most lost their families, they lost their brothers, sisters, parents, their spouses, their children. It was so sad and heart-wrenching. . . ."

Ann at the DP camp in Fürth, Germany. 1946.

Ann's Holocaust experience was different in at least one important respect: She had had the enormous advantage of having been with her mother and her sister while in hiding. Her father's tragic death was so painful that she had been unable to face it, but it was, she believes, her mother's profound love and constant support, even when her mother was ill, that gave Ann the strength to survive. For this reason, the immediate post-Holocaust period, such an agonizing time for the large majority of survivors, could more easily become for her an unexpected opportunity for a rebirth.

"For me, life took a different turn. It was exhilarating; each day brought new excitement. I was fifteen, ecstatic about being alive. I got to know young people at the place, boys. We danced to the tunes of the tango, and for the first time in so many years I allowed myself to dream about a glorious future that awaited me. I was so happy, full of life and expectations. I had a second chance at life, and I wanted to embrace it at its fullest."

Since material goods, including fabrics, food, and clothing, were in short supply in Tarnów (and throughout Poland), ingenious survivors began to travel to Germany, where they loaded their trucks with salable articles and brought them back to Tarnów. These items were then given on consignment to a number of merchants who tried to sell them at an enormous improvised flea market. Ann, though only sixteen years old, became a merchant. Because she bought selectively, and because of her energy and her intuitive knowledge of what would sell and what wouldn't, she became one of the best saleswomen at the market. She did so well that by the time her mother and sister returned from the hospital, she had earned a considerable sum of money and enough business acumen to continue to run the business, with her mother and sister as her partners.

They understood, however, that they could not live this way forever, and one year after their liberation Ann and her family had regained enough strength to make an important decision. They would leave not only Tarnów but all Poland behind them. It would be too painful for them to live with memories of their past and too dangerous for them to attempt to function and prosper in the midst of a hostile population. Since there was no future for them in their own country, they would look elsewhere. Their immediate goal was to reach the U.S. zone of Germany, from which they hoped eventually to travel to America, where they were certain that they would finally find a new and permanent home. Since refugees were not allowed to leave Poland, however, the journey to the American zone, where the DP camps had been organized, was dangerous.

"In January 1946, in the late hours of the night, we were smuggled into Germany. The truck was loaded with people. While crossing the border we were all very frightened and very still, my heart was pounding in fear of being caught, but we passed the border safely and continued our trip to the American zone in Berlin."

After about two months in Berlin, Ann and her family were assigned to a displaced persons camp at Fürth, near Nuremberg (the site of the historic Allied trials of war criminals, which were held soon after the war), in southeastern Germany. The camp was located in a poor housing development near a former Nazi airfield, and its buildings were small four-room stucco structures. Many displaced persons voiced—and still voice—numerous complaints about life in the DP camps, but Ann remembers, or wants to remember, only the positive aspects of her long stay at Fürth.

Living conditions were no more than adequate. Ann and her family slept on army cots and shared a kitchen with other temporary residents. As in Tarnów, this lack of comfort was of no importance to them. They had known much worse while in hiding. The presence of a barbed wire fence, which surrounded the camp, was also of no concern to Ann and her family since it did not remind them, as it reminded many others, of time spent in a concentration camps. In a DP camp, as opposed to a concentration camp, all residents were free to come and go as they pleased. There were no curfews or restrictions of any kind, and the only purpose of the fence was to keep nonresidents out of the camp.

Ann and her family remained in Fürth for two and a half years, from the spring of 1946 to the fall of 1948. If the time spent in Tarnów had opened the teenager's eyes to the possibilities of freedom, the time in Fürth completely energized her. She was vivacious and outgoing, dancing and partying with other young people, most of them lonely and, hav-

nprisonment, and four eceived prison terms ranging from ten to twenty years. three defendants were cquitted. On October 16, 946, eleven of the defendants sentenced to death ere hanged. Hermann öring, one of Hitler's most alued associates, took his wn life in his cell before he ould be executed.

Polish, Jewish, and other refugees protest together to improve living conditions at the DP camp. Ann is pictured at the front, center. Fürth, Germany. May, 1946.

ing been deprived for many years of contact with other young people, desperately eager to reconnect.

Ann's greatest concern at Fürth was education. The camp was very small—the population varied from about six to nine hundred during the time Ann was there—and was therefore unable to provide the basic schooling necessary to satisfy her immense desire to become educated. The camp was also unable to provide the educational and vocational training most of its residents needed to prepare them for their reentries into a "normal" world. There was little space for classrooms, a shortage of educational supplies, few books, no kindergarten programs, and no vocational courses to train auto mechanics, electricians, carpenters, seamstresses, or tailors, to mention only a few of the occupations that would be open to them once they were permanently settled. Most seriously, there were no qualified teachers.

Ann, having been robbed of formal schooling for three years, was undaunted. She took matters into her own hands and, in spite of all obstacles, made education the focus of her life at the camp.

"Without anyone's help, I found German professors to help me with my studies—I learned years later, to my dismay, that

these professors, the only ones free to teach me, were available solely because they were Nazis who were not allowed to teach in regular German schools. Had I known it at the time I would have had nothing to do with them. They gave me private tutoring, and in exchange for lessons I bartered with coffee and other food. I wanted to take everything in. In addition to studying English, Latin, German, geometry, geography, math, and literature, I took piano lessons—since I didn't have a piano, I used to go to a German woman somewhere outside of the camp to practice the piano, in exchange for coffee. Then I took horseback riding and dancing—that's something I've loved all my life. . . . These were the most happy times for me. Everything was so exciting. I loved being with people, loved dancing, talking, I loved life. . . . And after a year and a half, I was able to go to a German high school, outside the camp, to continue my studies."

Left: Ann's sister, Rae (left); her mother (center); and Ann at the DP camp. Fürth, Germany. 1947.

Below: Ann dressed as Charlie Chaplin at a DP camp Purim party. Fürth, Germany. 1947

As time passed, Ann and her family became restless and eager to leave the transit camp. Emigration to the United States, however, was then impossible. Visas to the United States were granted on the basis of nationality; the Polish quota, a small one, was filled, and there was a long waiting list. This meant that it might take years to be granted the necessary authorization. As an alternative, the family decided to emigrate first to Canada, the home of Ann's mother's brother, where they could await the papers that would enable them to live in the United States.

TONIA BLAIR left Poland behind and traveled to Berlin with her fellow survivors from Lodz. Their train broke down after crossing the German border, and only the intervention and reassurances of a kindly Jewish Russian soldier gave them the courage and the means to continue on to the capital. From there, in late December 1945, they were taken to a large displaced persons camp at Landsberg, some thirty-five miles from Munich. The small town, otherwise undistinguished, remains infamous as the site of the prison in which Adolf Hitler wrote his testament, *Mein Kampf*, in 1924.

At the time of Tonia's arrival in late 1945, the camp was dangerously overcrowded. The refugees occupied former German military barracks, which had been built for twenty-five hundred soldiers, but now housed forty-five hundred people. Another thousand DPs lived in seventeen houses and apartment blocks adjacent to the camp itself. Although a large majority of the residents came from Poland, others came from Lithuania, Hungary, Greece, and the Soviet Union. In December 1945 Jews constituted 90 percent of the camp's entire population, and during Tonia's time there, Landsberg became completely Jewish.

Conditions at Landsberg were initially characterized by overcrowding, underfeeding, and inadequate sanitary conditions. But as a result of the leadership of a dedicated physician named Dr. Nabriski (who became

A view of the Landsberg DP camp. Landsberg, Germany. 1945–1948.

a friend of Tonia's), the camp could boast of excellent medical facilities, including a well-run, well-equipped hospital. The schools, too, were considered unusually good. This was a considerable achievement in light of the difficulties most of the schools in DP camps faced: teachers who were inexperienced and frequently unqualified and students of various ages who came from different countries, spoke different languages, and had experienced the Holocaust in different ways.

The school system ran from preschool, where reading and writing were of the greatest importance, through college. More than seven hundred high school students enrolled in training courses for carpenters, electricians, auto mechanics, nurses, and other trades. In addition to these educational and vocational programs, there were recreational and athletic programs, but the main emphasis was on rehabilitation through education and work.

Landsberg was not, when Tonia arrived there, a typical DP camp.

Although it had in the beginning inevitably resembled the other hastily organized camps, conditions there had improved enormously, largely because of the enlightened leadership of one man, Major Irving Heymont, an American officer who assumed direction of the camp in September 1945.

Heymont was a man of sensitivity and of action. He recognized the quality of the medical and educational facilities, but he was disturbed by the crowded, unsanitary living conditions. He was also upset by what he considered the inhuman treatment of the emotionally damaged men and women who lived at the camp. The iron fence that surrounded the barracks had been increased in height by the addition of barbed wire, the symbol of the shame and ignominy of concentration camps. Armed soldiers patrolled the camp, and the residents, instead of fully enjoying their newly found freedom, could leave only with written passes, a strictly limited number of which were issued on a day-to-day basis. The irony of the DPs looking through the fence that enclosed them at the Germans who wandered freely through the streets of the town appalled Heymont.

The Landsberg hospital staff. Dr. Nabriski is sitting in the second row, center. Tonia is standing next to the man in the chef's hat. Landsberg, Germany. 1946–1947.

He took action at once. Passes were eliminated, and residents were free to come and go. Guards continued to patrol the entrance to the camp, but it was made clear that their purpose was to keep unauthorized Germans out, not to keep the DPs in. In addition, all traces of barbed wire were removed. Heymont's ultimate goal, which he worked tirelessly to achieve, was to give as much autonomy as possible to the survivors who remained at Landsberg while waiting to resume their lives.

Tonia remembers only good times during her year and a half at Landsberg. Perhaps the exhilaration she felt at being able to enjoy a relatively normal life in the company of people her own age so obscured the bad times that anything negative seemed unimportant and has been forgotten. Certainly, for many of the young people, Landsberg provided clubs and youth-directed activities for the very first time in their lives. There were two indoor cafés and an outdoor café. There was a thirteen-hundred-seat theater, a radio station that broadcast music and international news, and a camp newspaper. It was possible to have a good time there—in spite of the memories that plagued all the survivors.

Tonia also had a profession and no time to sit around and brood. Because of her training in the ghetto hospital, she became usefully and fully occupied, working as a nurse for twelve hours a day. She treated adults first and then children, and she did her work so competently that she was soon training younger nurses of seventeen or eighteen. On occasion she taught new mothers how to care for their babies. In addition, she lived in a dormitory next to the hospital, where she joined her colleagues in becoming part of one family.

"Since we were living at the camp, we weren't paid. . . . We had food and clothes. And we could go outside. I learned how to ride a bicycle, and I learned how to swim—Landsberg was on the Lech River. And I had admirers. I kind of looked down on the Polish, and for some reason, I took up with the

Tonia (first row, center) with friends from Landsberg on vacation at Berchtesgaden, Germany. 1946–1947.

Greeks. I remember we had fun, and there were the UNRRA people in uniform, and there were also soldiers, and we danced. They showed us films, too.

"We took vacations. We went swimming in the summer— there were no bathing suits, but we used pieces of cloth—and skiing in the winter. We even went to Berchtesgaden in the Bavarian Alps, where Hitler had a villa, overlooking the town. And we took a trip to the salt mines.

"Anybody you met said, 'Where were you? Who were you? Did you know so-and-so?' "

GEORGE SCHWAB found his way to Hamburg and to one of the most unusual and comfortable of DP camps, only a few months after the war had come to an end.

George shortly after liberation. Late summer, 1945.

Immediately following his liberation, he had remained at Neustadt in Holstein, the naval base that had been the site of his liberation and had been hastily converted into a DP camp. His stay at the improvised camp was interrupted by two hospital stays (he was in very weak condition) and by a short and very unhappy stay at a home for Latvian children, where he felt like a complete stranger (having spoken German at home, he never really identified with the Latvian language or culture). In the end he returned to Neustadt in Holstein, where he came to enjoy an easy life: He sat around talking and played basketball and volleyball and, most profitably, cards. This life, however, didn't satisfy him. An energetic boy not yet fourteen years old who had been prematurely forced into manhood, he was suddenly left to his own devices. He was determined to enjoy his newfound freedom. With more than enough money in his pocket—earnings from his cardplaying—and more than enough self-confidence, real or pretended, he ran off to the local railroad station and took the first train to Hamburg.

There, in September 1945, George was directed to an extraordinary DP camp. Located at Blankenese, a fishing village not far from Hamburg, the camp had been, in peacetime, a luxurious estate belonging to the Warburgs, an immensely wealthy and powerful German Jewish banking family. Built in 1796, and at one time an inn, the estate was a sprawling, comfortable place, with a coach house, stable, and garden. Members of the huge Warburg family—children and grandchildren—had gathered there each year to enjoy the pleasures of a summer in the country. During the war it had served as a military field hospital. When the war was over, the Warburgs had sanctioned the estate's temporary conversion to a home for between seventy-five and one hundred orphaned, homeless Jewish children.

Most of these children, between the ages of five and thirteen, had survived Bergen-Belsen, the notorious concentration camp where Anne Frank had died of typhus. They arrived at Blankenese underweight and

George (front) with friends at Blankenese, Germany. 1945.

neglected, many of them in urgent need of medical care, which the excellent staff was able to provide. The staff of about thirty workers included kitchen aides, cleaning women, night watchmen, seamstresses, and teachers (about one teacher for each ten children). These men and women, most of them displaced persons themselves, were able not only to provide these required services but also to offer the even more essential warmth, care, affection, and healthy and happy atmosphere these young people had lacked for such a long time and so desperately needed.

Education was a major priority for these children, who had lost years of formal schooling. Classes were held each morning from nine-thirty until lunchtime. Among the subjects taught were reading, writing, arithmetic, Jewish history, geography, and hygiene. There was also time for outdoor sports and play activities. Afternoons were largely devoted to games, gardening, nature studies, and arts and crafts. After dinner there were musical activities; the children could take music lessons and participate in community singing.

Jewish youths study Hebrew and the geography of Palestine in the Blankenese displaced persons' center for children. Blankenese, Germany. 1945.

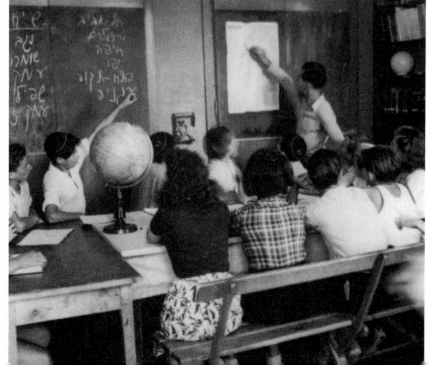

George remembers living conditions at Blankenese:

"I lived for a while in the main house on the third floor that used to be the servants' quarters, very nice. I remember that I shared a room with someone else, and there were maids' rooms up there and we all doubled up. That was the top floor. Underneath there was a private compartment within the complex, and there was an elevator. It must have been, before the war, a bedroom and sitting room for the Warburgs. And I think two of the people from the Joint, which administered the camp, lived there. And in addition there were one, two, three rooms facing the Elbe River. Nice large rooms where kids doubled up, and there was also a bathtub on the second floor, a bathroom. The toilets were separate from the bathrooms where we took our baths. But the main floor, when you came in, was wonderful, a hall leading straight into a large living room. To the right there was a smaller room and a bit further to the right was a large-size dining room overlooking the Elbe. To the left of the large living room were two rooms, probably a sitting room, a music room, maybe a library. . . ."

"While there we were being indoctrinated by Jewish soldiers. We were being prepared there for Aliyah Bet, illegal immigration, hopefully for legal immigration, but if need be we would run the British blockade and go to Palestine illegally. And we were being trained by soldiers of the Jewish Brigade, some of them in uniform and others not in uniform. Some of them came legally from Belgium—that's where they were stationed—and some of them were brought in illegally. Among other things, they taught us Hebrew (classes were taught in this language), they taught us the history of Jewry, and they taught us, they trained us for illegal immigration . . . in this beautiful setting, the Warburg estate. In the course of being prepared for immigration to Palestine, we also did a lot of gym, calisthenic exercise, running, et cetera, so that we would be in top shape. And we always heard stories about how the British interfered with the coming of immigrants, how we may have to land at night in order to evade them."

At Blankenese, George came to terms with his identity as a Jew and became committed to going to Palestine.

"Before the war I knew I was Jewish but I come from a very assimilated background. I knew when it was Passover—you eat matzoh then. I'd been to synagogue with my parents maybe only two or three times in my life. Not more.

"It was the war that radicalized me. During the war, I remember, I cried at night asking myself why I was being punished. What have I done? Where is my Papa, where is my Mama? Where is my brother? I didn't understand it. I was young.

"In time, of course, during the war, I came to understand that I was Jewish and by virtue of being Jewish, I was inferior. By

George's chauffeur stands by as George's friend sits at the wheel of the car and George leans against it. Blankenese, Germany. 1946.

virtue of being inferior, I deserved to be eliminated, to get rid of this Jewish scourge.

"Life was, in comparison to the first DP camp, beautiful on the estate. We did not lack food, we even had chocolate, we developed a great camaraderie among the children. And this cohesiveness was strengthened by taking meals together, welcoming the Sabbath, and after the Sabbath meal I was always looking forward to dancing the folk dances, because then you could invite a girl to dance with you, or the girl could invite you to folk dance. Of course, this was of great interest to me. Not only because of the folk dance but also because of the girls."

As time passed, George was able to make contact with relatives in England and, more important, the United States, who started bombarding him with packages and with money. This uncommon wealth enabled him to have a car and driver at his disposal during the daytime and also enabled him to sneak out of the children's home at night and go to Hamburg, a lively city only a twenty-five-minute subway ride away. There he could enjoy the pleasures of the city's nightclubs, pleasures usually not available to young adolescents under normal circumstances. He was, as he recalls it, having a good time.

It was through these relatives in England and the United States, and with the help of the Joint Distribution Committee, that George was able to make contact with his mother. George knew that his father and brother had been killed, but he somehow sensed that his mother was still alive, just as she felt certain that she would see her son again. The two were finally reunited in Berlin in May 1946.

"I knew I was going to meet my mother. We had been in phone contact, by way of military phones. Private phones.

Once a week we would talk on the phone. I thought to myself, my God. Here I am, a man of the world. I've been to Hamburg, this and that. . . . Now what will this lifestyle be again at home? I imagined this would be, once again, home with governesses, with maids, and drivers. I'm not used to it. I didn't want to. So when I was brought into the presence of my mother, I gave her a kiss—pro forma, I would say—and vice versa. She was a very strict woman, rather distant, but very, very loving—but you are you and I am I. I'm the mother and you're the son; you must always remember this. The first question I asked her was, 'Please tell me, Mother. What is the nightclub situation like in Berlin?' So she looked at me and said, 'Well, that's very interesting that you should ask. You know, I've been here in Berlin all alone now, a woman alone. Now that you're here we can explore it together.'

"I was satisfied with the answer. Subsequently, she told me when she heard this, she knew that she would have a problem on her hands. I was wild. . . ."

George and his mother shared one room in a small apartment in Berlin, and the boy almost wore his mother out, dragging her to three or four movies a day, taking the reluctant woman to cafés and night-clubs, and generally exhausting her. Finally, he was sent to school in a

On the way to America on the Marine Perch. George is in front, wearing a cap. Behind him stand Miles Lerman; Lerman's wife, Chris; and George's mother (right). Miles Lerman's sister, Renia Gelb, is kneeling at left. 1947.

DP camp in Schlachtensee, near Berlin. Though he was the youngest student there, he was put in the highest class because of his excellent knowledge of German. He also had a fair command of Hebrew and English. This time ordinary teachers, rather than the soldiers of the Jewish Brigade, continued George's indoctrination as a future immigrant to Palestine.

Since his days at Blankenese, George had become increasingly determined to go to Palestine to help build a Jewish state. But his mother urged him to postpone the move, convincing him that they should first go to the United States so that he might complete his education. George agreed. New York appealed to him; he remembered having seen a movie about the city before the war, showing fast cars and bridges that opened and closed quickly. They had relatives in New York. But most important, George had fallen in love with Shirley Temple and Bobby Breen, the child stars of his favorite movies.

ALICIA WEINSBERG and her family took several terrifying weeks to reach a DP camp in the American zone of Germany, after making their decision to leave Poland. The journey was planned and supervised by the Jewish underground organization Bricah. Since Poles were not allowed to leave Poland following the end of the war, secrecy was essential. There was always the fear of being caught by police or soldiers and taken into custody.

Alicia. Munich, Germany. 1946.

Part of a group of ten Jews, Alicia and her family were sent first to Kraków, where they awaited plans for their departure from Poland. The signal to begin their travels finally came after one month. They were told to go to Katowice, near the Czech border, where they were instructed to carry only knapsacks containing no personal items, such as documents or photographs, that might give away their true identities. They were supposed to be Turks or Hungarians, people going back home from concentration camps. They were also warned not to speak Polish, even among themselves. This was especially difficult for Alicia's nine-year-old sister, who was unable to speak any other language.

After crossing the border into Czechoslovakia, where they stayed in a special hotel for refugees at Bratislava, they went on to Hungary. They arrived there on Alicia's sixteenth birthday. There was time for a moment of celebration: "A few of the young men on this trip had already started being sort of my cavaliers, and I got perfume sets and all kinds of gifts. I remember it was October 2, and we were crossing the Danube River. It was a beautiful day. . . ."

Then their travels resumed.

"This time we were going to Budapest. All of this was directed by a group of these people. We were only given contacts—from time to time somebody came and said something. Like when we got to a station. At that time there were no schedules. There were no directions. A train came and you didn't know which train to take. At midnight I slept on the floor of railroad stations. And my sister by this time became terribly cranky. She was not used to this life, and I remember we found a toy somewhere, and that was something for her to play with. Generally, she was a very good child, but she was becoming impossible.

"Anyway, we finally got to Budapest, and then we spent a few days in one of the hotels. I remember we arrived there quite late in the evening, and the whole group at that time must have been about two hundred people. From the railroad station we were going to one of the places in the center of Budapest and walking with whatever we had on our backs, and some Jews that survived were running to us, asking where we were from, who survived, and where we were going. But they were trying to find out if anyone was from Hungary because the Hungarians were in Poland after the war, and they were coming back. In our group we didn't have any people like that, but it was very tragic to see how they ran after us, trying to find out who we were.

"We came to this place late at night. At that time it was very important to be at the beginning of the group, because as you entered the buildings you had to rush to find a bed for yourself. If you were in the back of the crowd, the chances were you slept on the floor because they were usually hospitals, empty hospitals, or old hotels or schools. They weren't equipped for this. . . ."

After Budapest, Alicia and her family were directed to go to Austria, which they reached only after several frustrating attempts. A number of borders had been closed, so they had to go from one to another. Finally they arrived at Vienna, where there was another brief, peaceful interlude: Alicia's father, who had lived and studied in the Austrian capital, was able to show his appreciative elder daughter the sights of his youth.

Alicia and her group then traveled by truck to Salzburg, Austria, and finally to Munich, Germany, in the American zone. They arrived in the middle of the night and were put up in the Deutschemuseum, a museum before the war (and again after it) but at the time a place of asylum, each room filled with beds, and with refugees. Having learned that a number of displaced persons camps were being set up around Munich, Alicia and her father traveled to one of the newest and best equipped, Fohrenwald, in the beautiful countryside a few miles from the town of Wolfratshausen. They registered, and soon afterward the weary family made the journey from Munich to their new temporary home. They were to remain in Fohrenwald for the next two and a half years.

The camp at Fohrenwald had been established in the fall of 1945,

Alicia's family's home at the DP camp at Fohrenwald, Germany. The family lived in the first unit to the right of the truck. 1946.

shortly before Alicia and her father visited it. Conditions at the camp, which had originally been built by the Germans for employees of a nearby underground armament factory, were considered very good. The refugees lived in small but comfortable apartments in central-heated, semidetached houses. The houses were built along concentric circular streets with the inner circle containing administration and community recreation buildings, as well as educational and vocational facilities.

Although Fohrenwald was originally designated as a mixed camp, bringing together displaced persons from all over Europe—Poles, Estonians, Lithuanians, and Hungarians, among others—it was soon decided, largely because of the hostility expressed by most of the non-Jewish residents toward the Jews, that it should be declared an all-Jewish camp, and the rest of the population was transferred.

Approximately three thousand Jews remained. About seven hundred of them were young people. It was estimated that there would eventually be room for some four thousand residents in all. That meant overcrowding was not a problem, as it was in most camps. The camp was not filled to capacity when Alicia and her family arrived.

Because of the fluctuating population, with residents coming and going, administration of the camp was extremely complicated. Though disease was rampant, especially among the new arrivals, the general health situation was reasonably good. The doctors were constantly alert to possible outbreaks of epidemics, especially among a population whose resistance to infectious disease was bound to be low. Hospital facilities were considered satisfactory, with a team of dedicated non-Jewish Hungarian doctors in charge.

As was the case in most of the camps, education was given a high priority. Schools were organized, and each young person up to the age of nineteen was required to attend classes. Those over fifteen devoted half their days to vocational training and the other half to academic subjects.

A great emphasis was placed on vocational training. It was impera-

"Open the gates to Palestine!"
Hebrew High School protest.
Munich, Germany. 1946.

tive that such training be provided for the young people at the camp, for they had had no chance to acquire any professional or vocational skills during the war. It was also essential for the adults at the camp to acquire skills that would equip them for the future. For this reason, there were training classes for nurses, tailors, hairdressers, carpenters, electricians, and other tradespeople.

The camp supplied food, which was, according to reports, somewhat inferior to that offered in nearby camps. There was little variety, and the meals were badly prepared. But it must be remembered that there were food shortages throughout Europe after the war, and gourmet meals were neither necessary nor possible. Although there was always a need for shoes, coats, and underwear, the camp provided clothing and blankets, which had often been donated by people in the United States.

Alicia was not interested in these matters. Her memories of the camp are happy ones. Most important for the energetic and enthusiastic girl, life at Fohrenwald gave her the opportunity to form friendships with other young people. For many years she had been unable to attend school or enjoy the company of people her own age. At Fohrenwald, opportunities for these contacts were plentiful. But for Alicia, an independent, headstrong girl, even these were not enough. She decided, after a short time there, that she no longer wanted to be confined within the limits of the DP camp. She no longer wanted to be fenced in, no matter how friendly—and protective—the fence might be.

"I decided I wanted to go to school in the city, and my father rented a room in a German family's house, and my girlfriend and I moved there and started going to school. This was a Hebrew school in Munich—not a normal Hebrew school because nobody spoke Hebrew or very little, and the teachers didn't know Hebrew, so they taught whatever they knew. They were not teachers. They were just people willing to teach whatever they knew. It was a wonderful time of my life, because we had a tremendous number of friends, food was given to us, nobody needed much. . . . We were free. We tried to catch up on everything that people lost. Luckily I had a family, but most of

A DP camp wedding. Alicia is to the right of the bride. Fohrenwald, Germany. 1946.

Right: Alicia waiting to leave for America. Bremen, Germany. 1948.

Below: Alicia, her parents, and her sister waiting to board their ship. Bremen, Germany. March 1948.

my friends were just alone and single and so forth, so my home was like a home to everybody. We started skiing and skating, and all these sports were open to us. We were very willing to learn and catch up on everything, but the most important was our social life.

"We just lived it up. We went from the morning to late at night, either opera or movies or a movie and theater, we were absolutely on the go—an excursion and skiing or excursion and dancing and summer things. It was two and a half years of unbelievable life."

CIVIA BASCH intended to emigrate to Palestine after leaving Romania in the late winter of 1946, but she never even reached the port of embarkation. Nor did she or other members of her group know where it was or how they were supposed to reach it. For their safety as well as that of the organizations and individuals that would help them on their clandestine flight from Europe, they were provided with no names, not even the names of the leaders who planned their journey or those who guided them along the way. It was a dramatic and frightening adventure for a young woman in poor health, who had been forced, without any preparation, to confront a new world alone. It was, she believes, her youth and her circumstances that enabled her to survive.

> "We were young. You can withstand an awful lot when you don't have an investment in someone you love, or can put someone in danger. That's why we were such heroes."

She and her companions from Oradea Mare began their trip by traveling through Romania and racing across the border in the middle of the night in order to reach their first destination, Budapest. While they awaited further travel instructions in the Hungarian capital, they were given information about Palestine and the Zionist cause. They were also sent to a farm outside the city to learn what they could about agriculture. This would be of special use to them in Palestine, where development and cultivation of the land would be of prime importance. At the farm Civia became sick. Diagnosed with pleurisy, she was carried by her companions, who refused to abandon her, on a stretcher to a nearby villa, where she could regain her health in order to resume her journey.

When Civia was well, the group returned to Budapest, where they were given detailed instructions about their next move: where to go and how to contact the nameless men and women who would guide them along the way. The adventure was fraught with danger from the moment they left Budapest. The journey took them from town to town for what seemed like days on end, until they reached the foot of the Austrian Alps. It was an experience Civia never forgot.

> "We scaled the Alps in the spring. It was very slippery, since the snow was melting. We had a pregnant woman and a seventy-something-year-old man, but we also had two Latvian Jewish boys who had deserted the Russian Army, and they were lifesavers. So we went through the forest. I guess the guards

THE DP CAMPS

must have been paid off, because we were told exactly at what hour to cross from here to there. The people who were our guides would leave us off in a certain spot, and then you were on your own until the next ones would pick you up somewhere in the forest.

"And then we scaled this mountain that people, you know, mountain climbers take big pride in climbing—with no gear whatsoever. And we had a couple of younger children, not babies but young children. . . . I tell you the truth, I don't really believe that I did that. It's like an out-of-body experience . . . I know I was there and I know I did it.

"We finally arrived on the other side of the Alps . . . I can't remember the name of the town. And we were told that when the train arrived to get on the train and forget about it. Don't say anything to anybody, and don't volunteer, if they ask you the names of the leaders, don't volunteer. . . .

Civia in a borrowed coat. Clug, Romania. 1945.

"We were a group of about sixty people, maybe seventy, from all over the world, from all walks of life, from all kinds of ages, and we arrive and we get on the train, and of course there are Germans standing, Austrians standing there. They can't get on the train because there's no room—it was a very small train. The conductors tried to get us off—we don't speak English, we don't speak German, we don't understand anything—and finally—this is the British zone of Germany—and if you think the Nazis were bad . . . Five o'clock in the morning the British came in with their bayonets and their guns, we could see their shiny shoes, all spit 'n' polish, and 'Get out, get out, get out!' and we didn't budge. And there was one young man who spoke English in our group, and they asked who the leaders are, so two idiotic guys volunteered. . . . They took them away instantly.

"Our saving grace was—you talk about miracles, we Jews live only for miracles—there was a Jewish guy in this British command, and he had some kind of rank, I have no idea what his rank was, and he came and he spoke to us and he said, 'Look, I guarantee you're not going to be punished, and you are going further, but these people must get on the train. There will be another train, and you will go. . . .'

"Well, finally, we're pretty stubborn people, but we finally went. What happened was they put us in a room, and the soldiers surrounded us like we were the worst criminals on the face of the earth. No regard for the Holocaust. It was such a long time ago, right? You know, I don't even know if they gave us food. I don't remember. I think they must have given us something. And I think we sat there for a day, and we finally got on a train, and that's how I think we got to Innsbruck, and pretty soon to what was a makeshift camp."

Civia remembers little about that camp, only that it was a very wide-open place, with some barracks in it. Nor does she recall how long they were there, only that afterward they were sent to Vienna, in closed boxcars. Civia was terrified; there were too many memories.

"Don't talk, don't breathe, don't cough, don't do anything. We were merchandise. It was back to 1944."

From Vienna, Civia traveled to Germany, where she stayed awhile in the enormous DP camp at Landsberg, where an organization to handle the immigration of refugees to Palestine had already been put in place. From there, she joined a group of fifty or sixty other young people who were sent to Konstanz, a town in the French zone of Germany, next to the Swiss border. There, night after night, trucks carrying four or five hundred youngsters on their way to Palestine stopped for food and med-

Jewish children from the Bad Reichenhall DP camp dance during their summer camp in Garmisch. Garmisch-Partenkirchen, Germany. Circa 1947.

ical attention at what had once been a Nazi camp for SS men and now was disguised as a fishing school.

Soon after, Civia's travel plans were once again thwarted by illness. A recurrence of pleurisy meant that she would have to be shipped back to a hospital in the American zone near Munich for further treatment. There her condition was diagnosed as tuberculosis. After a stay of a year and a half, she was transferred to Bad Reichenhall, near the Austrian border, where a large hotel had been converted into a sanitorium. While she was at this rehabilitation center, she received tragic news that changed the course of her life.

Civia had planned to go to Palestine because she wanted to be with a surviving brother, the person closest to her and the strongest link to her past. He had bought a visa for her on the black market soon after the war, but that visa was taken from her by members of the Bricah on the ground that the Jews of Palestine had more need for able-bodied men than for a sickly young woman. In 1948, when she was again preparing to go to Palestine, war had broken out there, and her brother wrote telling her to delay her departure until the conflict came to an end and he told her it was safe to come. She never heard from him again. While she was at the sanitorium, Civia was informed that her brother had been killed.

She was devastated. There was no reason to make further plans to settle in what had recently become the State of Israel. Instead she would go to America, where she had learned she had relatives. Though she had never met them, she had been assured that they would help her adjust to the New World in every way possible.

Once again, however, she met with difficulties and frustrations. In Bremerhaven, the German port from which refugee ships embarked for the United States, physical examinations showed that she still had scars on her lungs, traces of the tuberculosis she had suffered, and that her blood pressure was high. The diagnosis meant that she might not be healthy enough to work in America and could eventually become a ward of the state. This was potential grounds for denying her a visa. But she persevered. With the help of bribes—among them, five pounds of dates and ten Elite chocolate bars her brother had sent her from Palestine—Civia stubbornly pleaded her case day after day and overcame the bureaucratic obstacles placed in her way.

Jewish DPs living in wooden barracks in a camp in the Bavarian Alps. Bad Reichenhall, Germany. August 1948.

"I made a ruckus," she remembers. "I wanted to get out of this blood-soaked country." She insisted until she found someone in the immigration office to post the required ten-thousand-dollar bond that would enable her to obtain a visa. In the summer of 1949 she boarded the S.S. *Muir*, which took her to America.

LARRY ROSENBACH did not spend as much time in DP camps as others, and consequently they played a less important role in his postwar experiences. He reached a camp at Zeilsheim, in the American zone of Germany, several months after being liberated while on the death march to Dachau. He remained there for only six months.

The freedom Larry was about to enjoy involved making decisions, after so many years of having been given no choices at all and having been told exactly what to do and when to do it. For him, as for all the men and women who had been enslaved for so long, liberation meant, at the beginning, a fundamental transformation: from prisoner to displaced person.

It's certainly unlikely that Larry and his friends gave voice to or even considered these larger problems immediately following their liberation. They were in shock and able to think only of the present. Larry recollects:

"On the street somebody told us that there was a restaurant, and we should go over there and we would get something to eat. So we proceeded: We didn't know what to believe and what not to believe. We went into the restaurant and there were a few of our guys sitting at a table. Everybody was exhausted. In a few minutes this German brought out this soup. I took a few spoons of this soup, and it went down, and then I don't remember. I passed out or I just fell asleep on a bench. I don't know how long I slept. When I woke up I saw people near the windows, everybody was standing near the windows. I looked out also, and I saw American tanks passing by—maybe fifty tanks. Some of our guys went out to the street to greet them. I didn't go out, but the ones who went out, the soldiers were throwing K rations, and they were opening all kinds of cans and chocolate and whatever they had, I guess, when they saw how emaciated they looked. These guys gathered it, and they started to eat everything—bacon and whatever they got hold of. Most of them got sick from this food because they weren't used to eating something like this. And they went up to the hospital and I was told that half of us died in the hospital after the liberation because they allowed themselves to eat things they weren't supposed to. But I was lucky: I knew not to eat these things. . . ."

Toward the end of that first evening Larry and his friends, most of them no more than sixteen years old, were offered a place to sleep by a German couple.

"We were full of lice and vermin and everything and dirty. We were sleeping in these clothes for weeks and wet and muddy, so they took our clothes and let us sleep in the barn and the hay, and they took away the clothes and put them in the oven where they bake bread. Then they gave us our clothes back, and they brought us into their house. . . . And they tried their best to be nice to us. They gave us food that they sometimes didn't have for themselves."

After a few days Larry left his comfortable temporary place of refuge and set out to look for his brother, from whom he had been separated during the death march, shortly before their liberation. The search was difficult, but with the aid of a few fortuitous leads, the two were reunited in a nearby village, where they remained for almost two months. During those months Larry was, for the first time, able to savor his freedom. The townspeople were exceptionally friendly—possibly because they had been warned by the commanding American officer that if any Jewish survivor complained of being mistreated, the entire village would be burned down and the mayor (known to be a Nazi) hanged in the middle of the square. Best of all, the American Army provided the former prisoners with bicycles.

"We were riding around in the villages and the towns. We couldn't get over how nice it was to be free, with nobody to tell us we're not allowed to go there, you're not supposed to go. . . . We were drunk with this freedom. We enjoyed it like a dog you let off the leash."

Larry and the others of his group gradually began to prepare for the future.

"All we cared about was to gain some weight. There was a public scale, and we used to meet at the scale every day and jump on the scale to weigh. Everyone envied the other one—how much the other one gained. This was the whole discussion—you know, this guy gained two pounds already in three months, and this guy didn't gain anything. And this was our conversation and our wish—to get stronger and to gain. . . ."

Gaining weight, however, was only the beginning—actually a symbol—of rehabilitation, of the enormous changes that were taking place.

"Life was exciting because we had to readjust ourselves to normal life. I was in camp almost one-fourth of my life. I was thirteen when I went in, and I came out at sixteen, but even before the camp I wasn't living in normal conditions. We had always lived in fear, in degradation.

"After a few months, we had gained our strength, we had gained our weight, and we started to think about the future. We didn't know what happened to our families, we didn't know what happened—in general. We were detached from the world altogether. Nobody knew about us, and we didn't know about anybody else. . . ."

In spite of his feelings of isolation and loneliness, Larry and several of the young men with whom he had been liberated sought the advice of an American officer in the nearby town of Cham. The officer suggested that they go to the U.S. Army headquarters at Frankfurt, where they would be able to consult qualified army officers as well as representatives of a number of relief organizations that were stationed there.

Frankfurt was not easy to reach. Bridges had been bombed, few railroads functioned, and trucks and buses were scarce, but by following directions and taking advantage of any and all transportation available, the young men reached the city in a week.

After their arrival, in July 1945, the group was taken by army truck

Larry (bottom, center) and friends with the U.S. Army in Frankfurt, Germany. 1945.

to the suburban town of Heddernheim, an exclusive area where members of the Gestapo, the Nazi security police, had lived. They were immediately put to work by the U.S. Army.

"The whole area was just for Gestapo party members and their families, and they had all kinds of riches there. When the Americans came in, they gave them about four hours to clean out everything, so they had to leave a lot of valuable things—like pictures and furniture. And there was a piano in every apartment. The soldiers didn't need all this—they needed space because they wanted to put in as many cots as they could, and our job was taking out these expensive things, loading them on big trucks, and moving them to a dump, where they were chopped up, either to be thrown away or saved for firewood.

"After we finished doing these things for the soldiers, putting in the cots, their beds, in these rooms, we got different jobs with the army. We ate with them, got rations like the soldiers. . . . We had no complaints; they treated us very well.

"The only problem was when we ate, we were so hungry that we went twice, three times, to get food, something good like meat. Sometimes we would overdo it, and the soldiers resented the way we grabbed—until it had been explained that we had been inmates and were very hungry. But after a while, we got friendly with the soldiers, and we learned a little bit of English."

Larry. Frankfurt, Germany. 1945.

Larry enjoyed his time at Frankfurt. He and his friends worked at odd jobs—at the army store, the PX, and at a warehouse where they distributed clothing for the soldiers. They also did personal chores in and around the homes of the officers. Nonetheless, in spite of the comfort of this new life, and its sharp contrast with the Holocaust years, Larry

On the way to Palestine. Larry is in the center of the photo with someone's hands on his shoulders. Frankfurt, Germany. 1946.

became restless. He had been a free man for a few months, but he still felt as though he was merely marking time and postponing the decisions he would have to make concerning his future. He was totally unequipped for that future, and, having been brought up to believe in the importance of learning, he felt that to face it intelligently, he would have to complete his formal education, which had been interrupted after only four years. When a new displaced persons camp opened at Zeilsheim, near the army base in Frankfurt, Larry enthusiastically seized the opportunity to resume his studies.

The establishment of the new DP camp was a necessity. Larry was one of the first Jewish refugees to come to Frankfurt after the war, but in a very short time he was one of many; the number of homeless men and women in the city had grown to an estimated three thousand by the end of 1945. Because the new facility, which was supervised by UNRRA and the Joint, included a school, Larry decided to give up his agreeable life at the U.S. Army base and to move to Zeilsheim. The chance to resume his studies far outweighed the physical comforts offered by the army.

In many ways the population of the camp at Zeilsheim was similar to any "normal" town of three thousand, except that there were fewer children and old people. The Nazis, unable to use the old and the very young for labor, had killed most of them. In general, the camp had the diversity of age, educational background, and professional experience found elsewhere. There were doctors, dentists, nurses, educators, businessmen, manufacturers, engineers, auto mechanics, and farmers. In one way, however, there was a significant difference between the inhabitants of an ordinary town and of the residents of a displaced persons camp: Those who lived in the latter shared a common, and very disturbing, past. They had spent years in hiding, in work camps or in death camps, years of terror and anguish from which they would have to struggle to recover.

At Zeilsheim the former prisoners lived in German homes, which had been requisitioned in order to accommodate the inhabitants of the camp. This allowed family units to live together, in cramped spaces but with some degree of privacy. This was, of course, a luxury for those who had known no privacy for many years. Material conditions at the camp, however, were far from luxurious. There was a shortage of coal, and wood failed to give off the warmth required during the winter. Sanitary conditions were poor. Warm clothing was scarce, causing special hardships for the younger residents, and the food, barely adequate, was monotonous and starchy.

None of this bothered Larry unduly. He was young and strong and found great satisfaction in his studies. A Cultural and Welfare Committee, created by the Zionists, was responsible for the development of plans for educational and recreational activities as well as badly needed

On the ship to Palestine. Larry (age 17) is wearing a cap and standing in the front row, second from left. Marseilles, France. 1946.

vocational training. Courses were given in various languages (with an emphasis on Hebrew), history, and current events, and workshops were installed for vocational training. There was a weekly newspaper, a theatrical group, a jazz orchestra, a tailor shop, a shoemaking shop, a beauty parlor, and a barbershop, all of which provided services and trained apprentices.

Larry remained at Zeilsheim for about six months. In 1946 the British unexpectedly issued certificates that allowed one thousand Jews to enter Palestine, with first priority being given to young orphans. These orphans, most of them fifteen, sixteen, or seventeen years old, were selected from DP camps and schools throughout Europe. They were sent to the French port of Marseilles, where they embarked for their new homes in Palestine. Larry Rosenbach, homeless, without a family—his brother had chosen to remain with the U.S. Army in Frankfurt—and with no reason to go elsewhere, was among them.

JUDITH BIHALY was a small child, barely ten years old, when she began her postwar search for a new home and a new life. Because of her age, her memories of a DP camp and of her search, which also led to Palestine, are vague and incomplete.

Having been threatened and rebuffed by the occupants of her former home in Budapest, the frightened and bewildered child remembered the downstairs neighbors and, in desperation, turned to them for help. A Jewish couple who had somehow managed to escape the fate of the large majority of Hungarian Jews, they greeted her with the warmth she badly needed. They also gave her good news. Her twin brother was alive; he had been hidden in the country, together with their own son. Furthermore, they assured Judith that the organization that had arranged to hide the two boys would soon be able to place her in a temporary foster home in the countryside . . . but not quite yet.

Judith at a Zionist home in Budapest, Hungary. 1946.

"They couldn't take me with their car because I was crawling with lice, and they cleared the rugs and carpeting away from the floor so they could let me in the house. They didn't want me to touch anything that was made of fabric, because I guess that's where lice would . . . . They cleared a place and they put a wooden chair in the middle of the floor and they slid over, not wanting to touch me, slid over some bowls of food. I remember eating delicious food that they gave me. Looking back, I realize how sorry they felt for me.

"They attempted to use turpentine to get rid of the lice, but the lice would crawl out. I remember some of the kids in the building looking at me and yelling because my head was covered with a towel and the lice were trying to escape so they were crawling all over me. . . . But the eggs weren't killed, so the lice kept coming back.

"I remember this woman taking me, she was holding my hand and she was taking me and crying, she was taking me to a barber. They had to shave my head. I remember looking in the mirror. It was really like dying. I remember a Russian soldier coming in, I had long hair on one side and no hair on the other, and he was trying to be kind. He thought he was just making a joke, and he laughed at my head and said, 'Is this a boy or a girl?' I remember losing it. Anyway, I don't cut my hair now. . . ."

Under the direction of a relief organization, Judith joined a group of children—orphans or children whose parents had not yet been found—on a train ride to the countryside. They were met by families who were willing to offer them homes in exchange for help with various tasks, such as taking care of small children, doing chores around the house, or working on the farm.

After one mismatch—she was unable to satisfy the needs of a mother with a two-month-old baby—Judith was chosen by a woman who, miraculously, really wanted to care for her, not the other way around. The woman's husband was a Jew who had not returned home.

"She took excellent care of me. I remember her brushing the stubble that was my hair, so it would grow nice and shiny. I remember going to school there and everybody at the school paying a lot of attention to me, but in a very friendly way. I remember not wanting them to know me or to see me."

After about six months Judith was somehow—she's not sure how—reunited with her brother and mother. Her father never returned. She learned that her mother had been in Auschwitz, working as a forced laborer. She later learned that her mother had been partially blinded by fumes at work but managed to hide her blindness from the Nazis so that she wouldn't be killed. The three of them lived together in one room, which was given to them by the Joint.

At one point Judith and her brother were taken by their mother to a kind of hostel, belonging to a Zionist organization, where they were to live. It was an extraordinary experience for the young girl.

Judith and her brother, Andrew, dressed for the border crossing from Hungary to Austria. Budapest, Hungary. December 1946.

"When my mother said that my brother and I were going to live there—I understood that this was a Jewish place—I said, 'Yes, but I'm not Jewish. Can I still say my prayers?' My mother said, 'Yes, you can.'

"And when we went there to live, to stay there, I remember this enormous energy with everybody saying we're going to build a country. 'What do you want your name to be, your Hebrew name?' At that time I didn't know that Judith was a perfectly good Hebrew name. I don't know why they wanted to give me a Hebrew name; I already had one. I'm not sure they knew. I said, 'Yes, but I'm not Jewish.' They said, 'Yes, you are.' It was just a sudden transformation. It was like saying, 'Oh, so that's what I am.'

"It was a very important time in my life. It was like a turning point, but I didn't recognize it as a turning point; I had no realization of that until I spoke with my friend many years later. What happened was that I suddenly was living the life of a teenager. I was living there, bunking there, I had almost no social skills at all, but I loved participating in the Oneg Shabbat, which was Friday night dancing, learning Hebrew, learning Israeli songs during the meetings. There was so much going on, and every morning they would send us out on the streets to take the tram to go to school because by that time schools were open, and I remember taking my time and going into

Young displaced persons pose on a hillside with Castel Gandolfo in the background. They are waiting to move to the DP camp at Bari, Italy. June–August 1948.

classrooms after the school began, always being late, learning nothing. This was fourth grade. My school was interrupted in the third grade, and I was going to fourth grade—or finishing third grade, I'm not sure. Anyway, I remember falling asleep in class. I remember not understanding a thing that was going on and not really caring. To me life was back there, and I think . . . I remember being on the tram with other kids, and we had no concept of how to behave. I recall we were as rowdy as could be. We were just little animals."

On the night of December 16, 1946, Judith's entire Zionist residential group vacated the building and piled into trucks headed for the Hungarian border. Her mother, having volunteered to act as their nurse, joined the group. They all carried backpacks and knew that their final destination was Palestine. At night they left the trucks near the Austrian border, and, having been told not to speak, walked silently for what seemed like hours to the snow-covered border. It was Judith's twelfth birthday.

At the end of the walk the group was taken by truck to Vienna. About a week later they were taken to a DP camp in Germany. Judith doesn't remember the dates they arrived there or even the name of the camp, only that it consisted of a number of apartment buildings. She does recall that the group stayed together through all its journeys. They lived as they had in Budapest, with the same leaders, taking occasional trips to the countryside and also spending time learning about Marxism and life in Palestine.

Sometime during the following autumn they again boarded trucks and were driven to the Italian border in the Alps. Once again told to remain silent, they walked for hours in the snow-covered mountains. They had been warned to expect to be caught by Italian border guards but not to be afraid of them. Judith remembers the crossing as adventurous and almost joyous, and she also remembers that the border guards were, as expected, very friendly.

Judith (foreground) on an outing with an Aliyat Hanoar (Youth Aliyah) group in the Dan region of Israel. 1948.

They traveled through Italy to a Zionist home on a hilltop across from the town of Castel Gandolfo, sixteen miles southeast of Rome. It was a beautiful villa where another Zionist group, this one from Poland, also lived, awaiting their turn to go to Palestine. Judith remembers her mother's efforts to dissuade her—Judith was at this time not yet fourteen years old—from going on to Palestine:

> "She took several trips to Rome and began to talk about a wonderful DP camp she had discovered near Cinecittà, the movie studio where *Quo Vadis?* was being filmed. One day she announced that she had all along planned to go to America instead of Palestine but needed the Zionist organization to help her escape from Hungary. My brother went with her to the DP camp, but I refused. She made several attempts to abduct me, but the kids and the youth leaders of our group protected me, thwarting my mother's stubborn efforts to prevent them—our leaders—from 'kidnapping' me.
>
> "She didn't succeed. Sometime early in 1948, prior to our departure for Palestine, our group leaders gave my mother a false date of departure, by which time we were already in the southern port city of Bari, where we boarded a boat that carried Jewish refugees across the Mediterranean."

AKIVA KOHANE had been taken, along with other former prisoners, by American soldiers to the Austrian city of Wels, where an enormous armory had been converted into a temporary refugee camp. Upon his arrival he was faced with reminders of the tragedies that had befallen most of the survivors. Many of them were emotionally destroyed. Hopeless figures walked around naked, talking to themselves, completely out of their minds. Others were more fortunate; though irreparably damaged, they seemed

The first photograph taken of Akiva after liberation. Florence, Italy. 1945.

somehow capable, in time, of gathering the strength needed to embark on the long, slow, and painful road to what would at best be a partial recovery.

Akiva witnessed the rapid growth of the camp:

"All of a sudden it became international in that refugee camp. There were not only refugees from concentration camps, there was a big foreign population—people that were brought into Germany and Austria from Poland, from Ukraine, from Czechoslovakia, to work mainly on the German fronts to replace the Germans that were taken to the army. So they had not been in camps—they were like slave laborers, and they also ended up, most of them with their families, in that huge armory."

The task of repatriating and, often, resettling the many thousands of refugees who passed through Wels was daunting. They spoke different languages, they came from different cultures, and they had experienced World War II in different ways. Each man and woman had special requirements and desires.

The first steps in dealing with this diverse population of men, women, and children were taken by representatives from UNRRA and the Joint, whose task it was to interview, register, and classify them. The volunteers assessed the refugees' immediate situations and helped them plan for their future.

When asked where he wanted to go, Akiva immediately ruled out repatriation to Poland and instead expressed a desire to emigrate to the United States, where an uncle and aunt were living. Unfortunately, however, all efforts to reach these relatives—at an address in Brooklyn that his father had given him a few years earlier—failed, and without their help it was impossible to obtain a visa to the United States. (Because of

UNITED STATES IMMIGRATION POLICY

U.S. immigration policy regarding the victims of the Holocaust was far from compassionate in the years following World War II. Public opinion was generally against the admittance of refugees to this country. It was feared that these refugees would take jobs from Americans, especially from recently discharged members of the U.S. armed forces who were returning to their homes and in need of employment. There was also concern that many of the DPs were either Communists or Nazi collaborators and that too many of them were Jews.

In December 1945, however, President Harry Truman, sympathetic to their plight, ordered that the DPs be given preferential treatment under U.S. immigration laws. Unfortunately these laws, enacted in the 1920s, contained quota systems that discriminated against refugees from Eastern Europe, where most Jewish DPs had lived. For example, 6,254 refugees from Poland were granted visas each year, while citizens of Ireland and Great Britain qualified for 84,000.

A step in the right direction was taken in the fall of 1946, with the creation of the Citizens Committee for Displaced Persons (CCDP). This influential organization, headed by Earl Harrison and endorsed by some of America's most respected leaders (among its sponsors was Eleanor Roosevelt), was eventually supported by some 250 groups. In January 1947 President Truman asked Congress to authorize the entry of a far larger number of DPs into the country. Several months later a bill that allowed the entry of four hundred thousand refugees into the United States over a period of four years was presented to Congress. In spite of the vigorous support of the CCDP, the bill was the subject of angry debate and was not passed until June 1948. The version of the bill that passed was compromised and blatantly anti-Semitic, and it was bitterly opposed by Truman, who signed it only because it did allow for the entry of two hundred thousand DPs over the next two years.

In 1950 a new and amended version of the 1948 act, correcting the injustices of the original bill and extending the deadline for issuing visas to December 31, 1951, was passed and signed by the president. In the end, some four hundred thousand DPs were permitted to settle in the United States.

All told, more than one million refugees settled in 113 countries over a period of four and a half years after World War II.

the limited number of visas available to citizens of Poland, it would have been difficult even with their help.) It was not until later that Akiva decided on another possibility: emigration to Palestine. It was the most popular choice among the refugees, in spite of the difficulties and dangers one was sure to encounter in traveling there. His decision was the result of a visit by representatives of the Jewish Brigade.

Akiva was profoundly impressed by the proud, idealistic soldiers whose uniforms bore the insignia of the brigade and equally impressed by the sight of the tommy guns, submachine guns with the Star of David emblazoned on their handles, resting on the seats of the brigade's trucks. The idea of a powerful organization formed to fight for the Jewish people seemed to him incredible. Faced with insurmountable obstacles to reaching America and most eager, above all, to leave Europe and his past behind him, Akiva enthusiastically joined the large number of refugees who registered to go to Palestine.

Within a few days of his decision, he and the others began their momentous journey by truck to Italy and to an undisclosed port from which they would embark for their new homes. On the way they stopped at another refugee camp in Salzburg, Austria. There Akiva witnessed a chilling episode, an example of the inevitable, ugly, and understandable hunger for revenge expressed by a number of the newly liberated concentration camp survivors. He describes it:

"We were free, we could go out on the street, and we were just walking around, and a friend of mine—he was even smaller than me—was walking on the street just in front of the refugee camp, and in front of him were two other refugees from Hungary walking and talking to each other. This friend of mine, he was from Poland, but the other two were from Hungary. But they were talking Yiddish among themselves, and he overheard them saying, 'You see the other two guys across the street, they used to be guards in the camp.' So the little guy heard this and said, 'What? Why don't you grab them?' 'Nah, leave me alone, the war is over. I don't want to bother.' So he wasn't lazy, he crossed the street, grabbed those two SS men, who, of course, were wearing civilian clothing, he grabbed them, and he started to scream, 'SS, SS,' in the middle of the street in the middle of the day. And it was right in front of our camp, so everybody ran out and started to chase, and one managed to escape, but the other one was caught and brought to the camp, and they put him on the floor, and I have seen many things during the war but I have never seen anything like this. Everyone who was there was just going in and hitting this guy with whatever they could—sticks, hammers, with anything. Finally you couldn't recognize him anymore, he was like one piece of flesh and blood. Eventually the Americans noticed this and they sent

A short time after liberation. These are Akiva's friends with American GIs (he is not in the photograph). Wels, Austria. 1945.

the military police in and chased everyone away. They grabbed this guy and put him on the truck to the hospital, and I think they might as well have taken him straight to the morgue. . . ."

The refugees were taken from Salzburg to Italy for several reasons. The postwar Italian government was especially sympathetic to the plight of the refugees, and no concerted effort was made to prevent thousands of them from crossing the country's northern frontiers on their way to ports from which they could sail to Palestine. Furthermore, the social and political chaos of the early postwar years made covert operations relatively easy, and Italian authorities generally ignored the activities of the Mossad. Italy's location, too, made the use of its ports practical. Italy boasted a long coastline and was near the major concentrations of European refugees and relatively close to Palestine. Akiva was enormously impressed by the efficiency of the operation.

"We went towards Italy, and on the way we noticed there were a lot of other trucks joining us from different directions. When we approached the Austria-Italy border, it was night. They closed the canvas of the truck completely, and they said,

Akiva (center) at a DP camp near Milan preparing to go to Palestine. Tradate, Italy. 1946.

Akiva's group of liberated children at morning flag raising at Villa Bencista. Fiesole, Italy. 1945.

'Now be quiet, we are crossing the border.' And as we got there, I see guys, MPs on motorcycles riding around and speaking English, and all of a sudden they switch to Hebrew. We came through the border while the Jewish Palestinians were watching, across to Italy, and we got to Tarvisio, the headquarters of the Jewish Brigade, and we got off the trucks and we thought that we were in Tel Aviv. All road signs, everything was written in Hebrew. . . ."

Jewish DPs pitching tents on the pier in La Spezia harbor, where they are holding a hunger strike to protest Britain's refusal to let them sail to Palestine. La Spezia, Italy. April–May 1946.

The Jewish Brigade was remarkably efficient, too, in setting up facilities, most of them small, understaffed, and poorly equipped, but all of them somehow serving their purpose: to house the refugees as they traveled through Italy. Akiva passed through Bologna, where he slept in a park, and moved on to Modena, to an enormous camp, which was a converted military academy in which thousands of refugees were housed.

He was then part of a group of about one hundred boys and twenty girls—all under the age of eighteen—who were sent to a large villa in Vallombrosa, some twenty miles east of Florence. After almost a month there, the group was again moved, this time to another villa, in Fiesole, closer to Florence.

Akiva and the other young refugees spent a great deal of their time studying Hebrew, which was taught by some of the adult Jewish Palestinians staying in the villa. On Friday evenings the adults and the young refugees came together to sing and dance and put on shows. It was on one of these evenings that Akiva was befriended by a Jewish soldier, a young woman through whom he was able to find his uncle in America. However, before he was able to give his American relatives his address—this was a great problem since the movements of the Palestine-bound refugees were veiled in well-guarded secrecy—he was already at sea, braving the British blockade on his way to Palestine.

Jewish DPs camp out at the port of La Spezia while waiting for permission to sail to Palestine. La Spezia, Italy. April–May 1946.

The Survivors:
An Afterword

Previous page: A group of young Jewish women, rescued from Nazi concentration camps, walk along the waterfront of a resort town in Italy, where a settlement of 2,200 Jewish DPs was established with the assistance of the American Jewish Joint Distribution Committee. Santa Maria di Bagni, Italy. Circa 1946–1947.

The men and women whose stories have been told in this book are all survivors, not only of the Holocaust but also of the extremely difficult years following the Holocaust. During the post-Holocaust years they had to make enormous efforts to overcome the painful memories of their past (an impossible task to achieve, of course, but one that had to be attempted) and rebuild their shattered lives.

All these men and women ultimately settled in the United States, where they faced new challenges. These included a new country, a new language, new customs, and, for most of them, new professions to be learned and mastered. The fact that they were able to confront these challenges successfully is a tribute to their determination and their resourcefulness, skills they were forced to learn as a result of the Holocaust.

ALICIA WEINSBERG arrived in New York City in 1948 at the age of nineteen. An energetic young woman, she found it easy to adjust to life in her new country and had no difficulty with the English language, which she had studied while in Germany. In addition to continuing her studies at night, largely in the liberal arts, she found work: decorating windows, in various offices, and then, for many years, in the office of a French perfume house. She and her husband divide their time between New York City and Woodstock, New York.

CIVIA BASCH arrived in New York City in 1949 at the age of twenty-one. As promised, members of her family, though strangers to her, welcomed her enthusiastically. She was the first European refugee they had met, and they were

Civia. 1949

determined to show their love to this lonely young woman. Civia quickly learned English and worked at a wide variety of jobs—in a necktie factory, a novelty box factory, and a bakery—while pursuing her education at night. She finally found employment as a laboratory technician.

During her first years in New York she met a man who was to become her husband, and they moved together to Buffalo, New York, where she worked for the Erie County Health District. The birth of her two children made her stop working, but she soon resumed, eventually starting her own Jewish radio program and moving back to New York City.

GEORGE SCHWAB arrived in New York City in 1947 at the age of fifteen. A precocious young man, he breezed through high school and was graduated at the age of seventeen. He gave up an opportunity to study at Brandeis University on a scholarship in order to remain in New York, where he continued his studies and also reaffirmed his strong ties to the State of Israel. At first, he joined Betar, a Zionist youth group, and then Lehi, also known as the Stern Gang, another militant Zionist organization. In a short time he left Lehi, disagreeing with its rigid ideology and believing it had, after the establishment of Israel, outgrown its usefulness. A six-month visit in 1951 to Israel, where he found the climate intellectually and culturally confining, convinced him to make New York his permanent home.

He has had a distinguished career as a writer and professor of history at the City College of New York. In 1974 he cofounded the nonpartisan National Committee on American Foreign Policy, with the late Hans Morgenthau, and has served as its president. The influential organization, whose members include Arthur Schlesinger, Jr. and Henry Kissinger, is dedicated to what he calls political realism, a credo that holds that U.S. foreign policy should be driven by national security interests.

JUDITH BIHALY arrived in the United States in 1950, after spending some two years in Israel. She has written, "Without my conscious awareness, I was assembling myself into an identity I never had before. Some of me was silly, some thoughtless, but most of me was spontaneous and happy."

For this reason, she was despondent when her mother arrived in Israel to take her to America in the summer of 1950. But only a bitter legal battle could have prevented such a move, and young Judith—she was only fifteen years old—was advised not to fight that battle.

Judith functioned well in New York. After graduating from high school, which she attended at night, she learned to be a legal secretary. In the fall of 1953 she began attending night classes at City College. She had already, the previous year, taken ballet classes, and that later led to the practice of yoga. In 1976 she became a middle school math teacher, and in 1997 she became a certified yoga instructor. The next year Judith gave up her work as a schoolteacher, but she continues to teach yoga. She lives in Edgewater, New Jersey.

LARRY ROSENBACH spent a number of years in Israel before coming to the United States. Upon his arrival in what was then Palestine, in 1946, he worked for a while on a kibbutz, but he soon, at the time of Israel's War of Independence, joined the army. After leaving the military, he worked in a glass factory and studied to be a tool and die maker, but he was restless and unhappy for much of his time in the new state. In 1953, at the age of twenty-four, he managed to emigrate to the United States, where he finally found a home. His professional career has been a

Larry. 1949.

Working on the kibbutz. Larry is at the far left. Palestine. 1947.

successful one, first as a plumber and then as the owner of a plumbing supply business. He lives in West Roslyn, New York.

AKIVA KOHANE also spent several years in Israel. He, too, worked on a kibbutz at first, after which he served in the army, most of that time in the signal corps. Because of his experience in the field of communications, he was hired to build new telephone exchanges after his discharge.

Before long Akiva, eager to pursue his interest in electronics, decided to accept the offer of relatives in America to come to New York

Picking tomatoes at Kibbutz Alouim. Akiva is at the bottom right, wearing glasses. Palestine. 1946.

to study. The wait for a visa, however, was long. Obtaining a student's visa was impossible—he could furnish no guarantee that he would return to Israel—and it was more than eight years before he could obtain an immigrant's visa.

In 1958 he finally arrived in New York. He immediately found a job and at the same time began attending evening classes. It took him six years to complete his training, but during that time he worked in electronics and, later, with considerable success, in the motion-picture industry in New York, where he lives today.

In 1983 Akiva was one of the founders—and later a board member and treasurer—of NAHOS, the National Association of Jewish Child Holocaust Survivors, a New York–based organization that offers support groups, lectures, and video presentations to Holocaust survivors in search of assistance or information.

TONIA BLAIR was unable to secure a visa to the United States quickly. She decided to join her friend Bluma, who was traveling to South America at the invitation of members of her family, who had agreed to extend that invitation to Tonia as well.

Tonia spent more than two years in La Paz, Bolivia, and Rio de Janeiro, Brazil, before she was finally given a U.S. visa in 1949. After a stay in Florida with her uncle and aunt, she moved on to her final destination, New York. It was the beginning of an exciting time. "I went through my adolescence at the age of twenty-four in New York," she remembers. New York has remained her home until now.

Tonia's energy served her well in these unfamiliar surroundings. She embraced her new home and her new country with enthusiasm. She worked at a number of jobs: as a baby-sitter, as a doctor's assistant, for a billing company, for the Ford Foundation, and as a picture librarian at the National Council of Churches. She actively advocated American progressive political causes, and in 1954 she married Vachel Blair, a doc-

Tonia in New York City. 1950.

umentary filmmaker and the nephew of the midwestern poet Vachel Lindsay. She studied wherever and whenever she could: modern dance, painting, English, and Spanish; in Syracuse, where she lived for a short time, at Hunter College in New York, and finally at Columbia University, where she earned her B.A. in sociology in the spring of 1989, at the age of sixty-three.

ANN SHORE left Europe in October 1948 and traveled to Canada with her mother and sister. They remained there until 1954, when they obtained visas to the United States. Ann took advantage of her time in Canada to study, work, and enjoy a full social life, but New York, where she settled, soon became her true home.

Ann and her future husband, Sydney. Canada. 1953.

Once in the United States, Ann married and became the mother of three children; the first was born in 1959. During those years she became increasingly interested in art. She had studied painting at Sir George Williams College in Montreal, Canada, and later continued her studies in and around New York City: at Cooper Union, the New School for Social Research, C. W. Post College, and New York University, as well as with a number of distinguished private teachers. Her career as an artist flourished. She began to exhibit extensively and with great success in museums and galleries throughout the United States. She had also been the recipient of several prestigious awards.

Since the end of the war she had been determined to put her Holocaust experiences out of her mind and to remain silent about them. She succeeded in doing the impossible: She rejected the Hania Goldman of her youth and became Ann Shore, an American painter. "For forty years," she says, "I suppressed my dark past and embraced life with all the joys that it offered. I immersed myself in painting. Through abstracted images of nature, I created a world of transmutation and regeneration—sweeps and strokes of light-filled tones became my metaphor for celebrating the beauty of being."

For many years she was embarrassed by what she believed to be her mother's almost obsessive need to speak of the destruction of their town and of their years in hiding. Ann wanted to forget all this. She wanted to be like everyone else and not to be different. She did not want to talk, and she was certain that no one wanted to listen.

With the death of her mother in 1983, however, her attitude changed. She felt that it had become her responsibility to share her Holocaust experiences. She joined a support group, in which she talked about her life for the first time. She then realized that she and the other members of the group, as the youngest and last living survivors of the Holocaust, had an obligation to tell their stories publicly—above all, to the young people of today.

Before long she went one step farther: She became passionately involved in the planning and organization of a gathering of former hidden children. With the help of the Anti-Defamation League (ADL), the First International Conference of Hidden Children was held in May 1991 in New York City. More than sixteen hundred people from all over the world attended and shared their tragic experiences. Following the conference, the Hidden Child Foundation was formed, under the ADL umbrella. Ann Shore became, and remains today, the president as well as the heart and soul of this extraordinary organization, whose membership has grown to some six thousand from all over the world.

Through her many radio addresses, television appearances, and lectures in the United States and Europe, Ann has become a well-known spokesperson for victims of the Holocaust. She is a woman who after many decades found her voice and in doing so helped many thousands of others to summon the strength to face the realities they had hoped to forget, to articulate them, and thereby, to allow them to serve as a record of an unprecedented event that must never be forgotten.

*Ann at the
Hidden Child Foundation.
New York City. 1999.*

Acknowledgments

Obviously, I owe an enormous debt of gratitude to the men and women who courageously shared their memories with me: Civia Basch, Judith Bihaly, Tonia Blair, Akiva Kohane, Larry Rosenbach, George Schwab, Ann Shore, and Alicia Weinsberg. I learned a great deal from them—and not only about the Holocaust.

I am also grateful to many others, who contributed to this project in many ways: George Alexander, Eva Blaikie, Donna Briggs, Riane Gruss, Eva Hirschenstein, Dr. Alexander Kirschenbaum, Elihu Kover, Gina Lanceter, Carla Lessing, Suzanne Rosenthal, Louis Schneider, Simon Schochet, Stefanie Seltzer, Rae Weitz, and Isaac Willner; Joan Ringelheim, Judith Cohen, Arven Donohue, and Martin Goldman, of the United States Holocaust Memorial Museum; Eric Nooter and Amy Shuter, of the American Jewish Joint Distribution Committee, and Ava Weiss and Phyllis Larkin, of Greenwillow Books.

Authors often complain that there are no good editors anymore, but Virginia Duncan and Susan Hirschman of Greenwillow Books are proof that this is most certainly not true, and I enthusiastically thank them.

Norma Jean Sawicki—as editor, publisher, and friend—encouraged me when I first expressed interest in writing a book about the Holocaust and published my first one. Her advice and friendship have been invaluable to me for many years.

Maria Rosenbloom has been generous with her uniquely perceptive and intelligent suggestions whenever needed, and I am grateful to her.

My wife, Paola, and my son, Daniel, have been unfailingly supportive, in every way and at all times, and I hope I don't have to tell them how much that support has meant to me.

Finally, I am deeply grateful to Gabriele D. Schiff for unselfishly sharing her profound knowledge of the post-Holocaust years as well as her personal experiences in the DP camps. She is a woman of great sensitivity and intelligence, and it would have been very difficult to write this book without her guidance.

For Further Reading

Bauer, Yehuda. *Out of the Ashes*. Oxford: Pergamon Press, 1989.

Berenbaum, Michael. *Witness to the Holocaust*. New York: HarperCollins, 1997.

Dawidowicz, Lucy S. *The War Against the Jews, 1933–1945*. New York: Holt, Rinehart and Winston, 1975.

Dinnerstein, Leonard. *America and the Survivors of the Holocaust*. New York: Columbia University Press, 1982.

Dwork, Debórah. *Children with a Star: Jewish Youth in Nazi Europe*. New Haven: Yale University Press, 1991.

Epstein, Helen. *Children of the Holocaust*. New York: Viking Penguin, 1988.

Friedlander, Saul. *When Memory Comes*. New York: Farrar, Straus and Giroux, 1979.

Gilbert, Martin. *The Holocaust: A History of the Jews of Europe During the Second World War*. New York: Holt, Rinehart and Winston, 1985.

Haas, Aaron. *The Aftermath: Living with the Holocaust*. New York: Cambridge University Press, 1996.

Langer, Lawrence L. *Holocaust Testimonies: The Ruins of Memory*. New Haven: Yale University Press, 1991.

———. *Preempting the Holocaust*. New Haven: Yale University Press, 1998.

Levi, Primo. *Survival at Auschwitz* (originally *If This Is a Man*). New York: Collier Books, Macmillan Co., 1959.

Meltzer, Milton. *Never to Forget: The Jews of the Holocaust*. New York: Harper & Row, 1976.

Moskovitz, Sarah. *Love Despite Hate: Child Survivors of the Holocaust and Their Adult Lives*. New York: Schocken Books, 1983.

Rabinowitz, Dorothy. *New Lives*. New York: Knopf, 1976.

Rosenberg, Blanca. *To Tell at Last: Survival Under False Identity, 1941–45*. Urbana and Chicago: University of Illinois Press, 1993.

Rosenbloom, Maria Hirsch. "What Can We Learn from the Holocaust?" *Jewish Social Studies Program*. New York: Hunter College, 1996.

Sachar, Abram L. *The Redemption of the Unwanted*. New York: St. Martin's/Marek, 1983.

Schiff, Gabriele. "The Legacy of Displaced Persons: A Personal Chronicle," *Journal of Jewish Communal Service*, vol. LVI, no. 4 (Summer 1980): 310–315.

Schochet, Simon. *Feldafing*. Vancouver: November House, 1983.

U.S. Holocaust Memorial Museum. *1945: The Year of Liberation*. Washington, D.C.: 1985.

Note: For an extraordinarily moving evocation of the Holocaust, I recommend the two volumes of *Maus*, by Art Spiegelman, published by Pantheon (New York) in 1986 and 1991. Using the form of a cartoon strip to recount the story of his father's survival during and after the Holocaust, Spiegelman makes a unique contribution to the literature of those years.

* *For more information about the Holocaust, World War II, and the post-Holocaust years, please visit the United States Holocaust Memorial Museum at 100 Raoul Wallenberg Place, Washington, D.C. 20024 www.ushmm.org*

Notes

1. From "Landsberg Revisited" by Samuel Bak, *Dimensions*, vol. 13, no. 2 (1999): 31–36. Reprinted with permission of the Anti-Defamation League.

2. From "The Legacy of Displaced Persons: A Personal Chronicle" by Gabriele Schiff, *Journal of Jewish Communal Service*, vol. LVI, no. 4 (Summer 1980): 310–315.

Photo Credits

The author and editor wish to thank Judith Cohen and Christopher Sims at the United States Holocaust Memorial Museum Photo Archives for their invaluable assistance with the photo research for this book.

Permission to reprint photographs is gratefully acknowledged to the following:

Pages vii, 104, 134: Civia Basch

Pages vii, 19, 116, 118, 120: Judith Bihaly

Pages vii, 40, 41, 43, 87, 89, 137: Tonia Blair

Pages vii, 45, 46, 122, 125, 126, 127, 136 (bottom): Akiva Kohane

Pages vii, 30 (both), 31 (all), 34, 111, 112, 113, 115, 135 (bottom), 136 (top): Larry Rosenbach

Pages vii, 25, 90, 91 (top), 93, 95: George Schwab

Pages vii, 6, 7, 8, 9, 79, 80, 83, 84 (both), 138, 139: Ann Shore

Pages vii, 13 (both), 15, 96, 99, 100, 101, 102 (both): Alicia Weinsberg

Pages xiv–1: Francis Robert Arzt, courtesy of USHMM Photo Archives

Pages 4, 70: National Archives, courtesy of USHMM Photo Archives

Page 28: USHMM Photo Archives

Page 38: Lydia Chagoll, courtesy of USHMM Photo Archives

Pages 52–53: State Archives of the Russian Federation, courtesy of USHMM Photo Archives

Page 56: Yad Vashem Photo Archives, courtesy of USHMM Photo Archives

Page 57: Ruth Gruber

Page 65: Bettmann/Corbis

Pages 66–67: Gina Hochberg Lanceter, courtesy of USHMM Photo Archives

Page 75: Irving Heymont, courtesy of USHMM Photo Archives

Page 86: Herbert Friedman, courtesy of USHMM Photo Archives

Page 91 (bottom): Beit Lohamei Haghettaot, courtesy of USHMM Photo Archives

Page 106: Rochelle Szklarski Shulman, courtesy of USHMM Photo Archives

Pages 107, 130–131: American Jewish Joint Distribution Committee, courtesy of USHMM Photo Archives

Page 119: Judith Bihaly, courtesy of USHMM Photo Archives

Pages 128, 129: Sarah Fiszman Saaroni, courtesy of USHMM Photo Archives

Index

Page references to photo captions are in *italics*.